W9-BDS-425

Family, Community, and Higher Education

This book explores social topics and experiences that illustrate the various ways in which the family unit influences and impacts college students. In the text, the authors not only explore family memories, but also challenge the traditional lack of inclusion and appreciation for "family" as knowledge producers and educational allies. This book spotlights the family unit as a critical factor within the educational experience—one that prepares, supports, and sustains educational achievement through both everyday simple lessons and critical and difficult family challenges. Through these experiences, families teach the lessons of survival that often help students to persist in college.

Toby S. Jenkins is Assistant Professor of Higher Education and Integrative Studies at George Mason University.

Routledge Research in Education

For a full list of titles in this series please visit www.routledge.com

Family, Community, and Higher Education

Edited by Toby S. Jenkins

Routledge
Taylor & Francis Group
NEW YORK   LONDON

First published 2013
by Routledge
711 Third Avenue, New York, NY 10017

Simultaneously published in the UK
by Routledge
2 Park Square, Milton Park, Abingdon, Oxon OX14 4RN

*Routledge is an imprint of the Taylor & Francis Group,
an informa business*

Library of Congress Cataloging-in-Publication Data

    Family, community, and higher education / edited by Toby S. Jenkins.
       p. cm. — (Routledge research in education ; 89)
    Includes bibliographical references and index.
  1. Community and college—United States. 2. Home and school—
United States. I. Jenkins, Toby S. (Toby Susann), 1975–
    LC238.F36 2012
    378.1'03—dc23
    2012029947

ISBN: 978-0-415-50227-6 (hbk)
ISBN: 978-0-203-07180-9 (ebk)

Typeset in Sabon
by IBT Global.

Printed and bound in the United States of America on sustainably sourced
paper by IBT Global.

To my parents, grandparents, sister, aunts, uncles, cousins, brother-in-law, nieces, nephew and all of those "fake aunts" and "play cousins" who taught me the meaning of family.

Contents

Introduction
Family First

Toby S. Jenkins

Many years ago, I read W. E. B. Dubois's classic text *The Souls of Black Folk* (1903) for the first time. Of course the book as a whole is an incredible work of critical social thought, ethnographic research, and cultural analysis. But the chapter that most deeply spoke to my consciousness was the essay, "Of the Meaning of Progress." In this chapter, Dubois relates his experience serving as a teacher at a local colored school in the South. This was a farming and sharecropping community. "School" was seen as both a necessary vehicle to escape oppression and an inconvenient distraction from the daily work needs of the community. Although parents wanted their children to attend school, they needed their children to help with the farming. Life trumped dreams every time. But even still, although many families often pulled their children out of school for short stints during heavy work times on the farm, as a community, these families were dedicated to the *idea* of their children being educated. They were so dedicated that they collectively provided room and board to the community teacher to ensure he remained in the community and that school remained an option. These families welcomed DuBois into their homes, fed him, and basically gave whatever resources they had to support education. This type of fellowship between the teacher and the families of students was striking. DuBois was more than an educator, more than a community member—he literally became a part of many of these families. And so his relationship with and understanding of the unique cultural dynamics that existed within this community helped him to be a successful teacher. As an educator, he was constantly challenged not to expect or force families to conform to his idea of commitment, participation, or structure. Time and again, he found himself putting feet to dirt road to personally visit a family whose child hadn't been in school for a while. He was consistently pushed to acknowledge and deal with the real impact of poverty on people's lives. The stress of struggle and oppression doesn't stop simply because a school bell rings. Young people bring with them into classrooms and onto college campuses histories—histories of community, family, heritage, love, struggle, poverty, abundance, addiction, resilience, pride, and shame. They bring to us their real lives. And too often we unintentionally disregard who they were and who they are in order to focus on what they are to become. Our vision within education must not be in one direction, looking forward. To truly understand and serve our students we need to appreciate all of the views that we can take of a person's life—look in the rearview mirror to see clearly their life history, use peripheral vision to catch glimpses of problems and issues that may not be in your direct sight. In other words, we need to do more than look at and examine students—we need to look into them— into their lives, their families, and their souls.

This book offers such a glimpse into the lives of people of color—undergraduates, graduate students, college graduates, and parents. Their stories illustrate the ways in which the personal consistently intersects with the professional. All of the authors spend time reflecting on the roles that their families played as the first and most sustaining educators in their lives. Too often we privilege those holding professional positions with the title of "teacher," "educator," "scholar," or "genius." However, these stories show that the most enduring lessons taught to most of us did not take place in a college classroom or within a co-curricular leadership experience. Many of these life-long lessons come from home—the very place from which the act of going to college often disconnects students. I first thought to offer a book on family and college after completing a study on the meaning and utility of culture in the lives of college students of color. Overwhelmingly, across racial and ethnic lines, socioeconomic status, and geographical region, family was always named as the most important marker of culture. At the time, I was serving as director of the Paul Robeson Cultural Center (PRCC) at Penn State University. This study caused me to pause and consider our approach to cultural programming. If students named family as the most important marker of culture, how were we including family both physically and philosophically into our programs? I was ashamed that for many of these students whom I loved like members of my own family, I didn't even know their mother's name. So many of the students coming from single parent households expressed deep love, respect, and regard for their mothers. Most often, she was the reason that they were in college. How dare we separate her from the experience for which she has worked so hard and sacrificed so much to give to her child.

I now cringe when I hear terms like "helicopter parents." Familial involvement is often seen as an enemy of the state on a college campus. Most often the marker for healthy campus adjustment is when students stop constantly going or calling home and are fully integrated into their new campus community. When parents, who have been advocates, allies, sponsors, and partners in their child's education for 13 years (including pre-school), exhibit pure excitement and a desire to continue to be an involved and active participant in this new phase—we close the gates and hang a FERPA sign on the rails. There has to be another way. Many colleges and universities do not hesitate to welcome parents into the fold as *donors*. Often many parents find their identity being changed from partner to paycheck.

Although many students may feel that they are just a number at an institution, many parents often feel that they are just a dollar sign. We must do better. We must envision creative ways to establish a balanced and healthy space for parents in the college experience. While pushing young adults to learn independence, make smart decisions, take responsibility for their lives, and manage their own affairs, we can also create a space where families can continue to participate, love, and support this growth. We can also do more to integrate opportunities to intellectually wrestle with family life and personal experiences in college. We can make a student's family experience a topic for discussion in a classroom or the focus of a co-curricular experience. After conducting that original study, I began to lead a change in the structure and content of some of our cultural programs in the cultural center. I co-created a feminist arts retreat with my colleague Crystal Endsley. The overarching purpose of this retreat was to acknowledge mothers in particular and families in general as producers of critical knowledge. We had a small group of men and women select either a tablecloth or an apron to serve as their artistic canvas. We called the aprons and tablecloths materials of resistance, as we chose to use some of the very items that have been associated with women's oppression to serve as a space to resist the idea that mothers, housewives, parents, or nurturers are not intelligent, skillful, and important members of our society. But what is most salient about this retreat is that rather than facilitating it ourselves or inviting a national artist or scholar to lead the session we invited our own mothers to facilitate the retreat. Neither of our mothers had ever attended college and both were tickled to be asked to "teach" college students. I overheard my mother on the phone with one of her friends excitedly sharing the news, "Girl, you know I've been asked to come to Penn State to teach a college class!" Our mothers may not have seen themselves as traditional college educators but my colleague and I saw our mothers as geniuses. They were experts of their own experience—her mother made quilts and my mother painted aprons as a hobby. These women were artists in their own right, creating beauty from their bare hands. But most importantly when we looked back at our lives and the critical lessons that made us into academics we clearly understood that it was their voice that we remembered—not a teacher or an administrator. We wanted to personally model this value for family to our students. We had each student paint the politics of survival and critical life lessons that they had learned from their families onto their tablecloth or apron. Space to reflect on their real life experiences outside of the college campus is critically important to help students mature into fully functioning adults not just skillfully prepared professionals. What was shared was awe-inspiring. Their appreciation for their families, honest sharing of good times, admission of dysfunctional family units, and reflections on the challenges of being an orphan taught all of us something about culture and family. Prior to hiring a graduate assistant, Samuel Lopez, who had spent the majority of his life in and out of foster care and group homes, I had rarely considered the unique experiences of college students coming from foster care, lives as orphans, or homeless situations. Even though we might fail to adequately include families, we often still assume that everyone has one. On his apron, Sammy painted the city of New York—its famous buildings and sites. Each item on his apron represented all of the places that he wished he had been able to go with his mother, who was killed when he was very young. But even more, he shared that the city itself represented his family—the city, the streets of New York had been his family and had raised him for much of his life. That's real. Guiding a young person that didn't have a family unit helped me to truly understand the real meaning of progress. In the past I had simply appreciated it, but now I lived it because I was called to become more than a mentor or educator—I needed to be family. You see advancement in life means very little if it is not rooted in a loving community that can celebrate and be proud. And so my staff and I, and my colleagues and dear friends within the broader field of higher education, have worked intentionally to create a loving and supportive family network for Sammy. When he and his wife recently gave birth to a daughter, I made the 4-hour drive to the Bronx to kiss that baby because I care about more than Sammy's professional achievements—I care about his life. That's what families do.

And that's what we must do. We must embrace the very idea of family. Because how we demonstrate regard for students' families and communities will influence how they view their own communities as they persist through college. Too often, I hear students come back from a break frustrated that they no longer can identify with "home." The thought is "no one understands me there." But perhaps the real issue is that college isn't helping the student to better understand the community. We need a new vision for higher education—one that compels us to help students to appreciate and commit to helping their home communities. The only phrase that makes me cringe more than "helicopter parents" is the saying "making it out of the ghetto." I detest the ways that our society, through schools, corporate institutions, popular culture, and political parties, situates "success" as residing as far away from impoverished communities as possible. Because we encourage the students from these communities that exhibit potential to make it out—get out and don't look back—we contribute to the cycle of oppression in their communities. Of course none of us want to live in a place where our lives are at risk. Everyone that works hard for a college education wants to enjoy the rewards of it. But there is deep value in creating blended socioeconomic communities—places where young poor kids can be inspired by their college educated neighbor. In addition, middle class money brings middle class resources to communities. Development follows dollars. This issue is important to me because it is personal. Although I am now a professor at George Mason University in northern Virginia, I was raised in Columbia, South Carolina. I consider myself a community daughter of Columbia. Similar to the giant oak trees that are found throughout my home state, no matter how far and wide my branches grow, I am always rooted in the soil of South Carolina. And so many years ago, as a college educator, I also found myself coming home for school breaks. And I began to see my community with new eyes. I saw a perimeter of poverty with clear borders that engulfed my old neighborhood. Crime was pervasive. Unemployment was high. There was no healthy commercial infrastructure in the community—the only businesses in walking distance were fast food chains, pay day loan companies, and liquor stores. You had to drive 20 minutes to eat healthy but most folks in my neighborhood walked or rode the bus—a car is a privilege. Rather than looking at my community with shame and vowing not to come back and visit as often, I decided to invest there. I went in the unconventional direction toward my neighborhood rather than away from it. My thought was "we" have to do something. If those of us that were raised in impoverished communities don't feel a sense of commitment to our home communities, then we probably shouldn't expect others to care either. Who I am and what I've become is not only a result of the schools that I attended and the professional experiences that I have had, but also what I learned in the neighborhood where I was raised in Columbia. I felt a responsibility to help my community because I do have good memories of good people there. I will never forget how big of a deal it was to my neighbors when I graduated from college and accepted a job in Madison, Wisconsin, with Oscar Mayer Foods. The morning that I flew out to move to Madison, my neighbors woke up at 6 a.m. to stand on their porches and wave goodbye. I am where I am and who I am because of the working class folks that loved me. And so, I bought a house in my old neighborhood as a start to a bold idea to help raise up the community that raised me. I began meeting with the neighborhood association and local politicians to learn more about community development opportunities. And I have more recently been working on a project that will tie my work at George Mason University with my work in South Carolina by bringing college students to work collaboratively with the community on transformation efforts as a credit-bearing field based course. I share this story because its spirit is really the point of it all. I conceptualized this book because I value cultural and community rootedness. A sense of rootedness will be explored throughout this book by examining the ways that higher education can either kill or nurture the community and family roots that are planted prior to college attendance.

This book is a book of stories. We learn to love stories at a very early age. Stories teach moral lessons, share knowledge, and pass on values. They provide us with a context to better understand complex issues or broad concepts. Stories help us to make sense of the meanings of life experiences. According to Banks-Wallace (2002), storytelling, the interactive process of sharing stories, is a vehicle of preserving culture and passing it on to future generations. Allowing people an opportunity to truly reflect on their experiences—to get to the root of their culture—is an important act of self-understanding and rebellion against negative social ideas. Smiley (2006) points out that story-telling and reflection have a critical role to play in community action and cultural sustainability. He describes reflection as "the deliberate process of taking your actions into account, examining them, learning from them, and then adjusting your future actions in accordance with the lessons learned" (p. 62). The reflection shared through stories helps to sustain a sense of self—a proof of existence and history. Featherstone (1989) has noted the value of the use of storytelling to inform research. He explains both the rich-ness and complexity of the information gained through story as well as the significant responsibility of the researcher.

> The telling of stories can be a profound form of scholarship moving serious study close to the frontiers of art in the capacity to express complex truth and moral context in intelligible ways. . . . The method-ologies are inseparable from the vision. Historians have used narrative as a way in which to make sense of lives and institutions over time, but over years they have grown abashed by its lack of scientific rigor. Now, as we look for ways to explore context and describe the thick textures of lives over time in institutions with a history, we want to reckon with the author's own stance and commitment to the people being written about. Storytelling takes on a fresh importance. (p. 367)

And so, each chapter in this book is a personal story and the authors come from various backgrounds: current college students, higher education professionals, and private sector professionals. I have also invited members of my family—my brother-in-law and my niece—to participate in this book. I try to use every opportunity to include my family in my work. Although it is typical to focus higher education texts on the student or academic voice, I decided to also include parents and working professionals in order to illus-trate the lasting impression of families—to, through, and beyond college. The idea to include professionals occurred to me when I was in the prep room waiting to undergo surgery for breast cancer. Dr. Stephanie Akbari is a renowned breast surgeon and the head of the Virginia Hospital's Breast Center in Arlington, Virginia. She was recently named one of the top breast surgeons in the DC area by *Washingtonian Magazine*. She is accomplished. But the signature pieces of her personal practice are the handmade pillows that she delivers to each of her breast cancer patients just before surgery. As she hands over a little gift bag she says, "My mom made this for you." Her mother personally sews a handmade comfort pillow for each of her daugh-ter's patients . . . a pillow to soothe armpits, breasts, or backs that need to heal after surgery. When she gave me my pillow my eyes watered and I locked eyes with my own mother because at that moment I knew she was the right doctor—family also meant everything to her. She loved and included her mom in her work just as I did. Much later, I was moved by a story that my friend Gay shared with me about his most salient college memory. Gay was a football player who was fully engaged in the college experience—outside of the classroom. One semester his grades slipped (during the time when grade reports were still sent home). His father received the report. He explained that his father never drove long distances and rarely traveled. His father had only been to one of his football games during his entire college career—the one in the state of Florida where they lived. His dad's infrequent attendance was not due to a lack of support; Gay was playing college ball to please his father. But on this day, when his father got the grade report he got in the car and drove from Florida to South Carolina to speak directly with his son. Gay was on the field at practice when the coaches called him to their office and informed him that his father was there. He felt shock and fear. His father had never been to his school. But he drove there because his son needed a parent. They talked about priorities and that academics trump sports—at least in their family. You see, Gay is a third-generation college student—he, his father, and his grandfather all attended college. Three generations of African American men dedicated to higher education—a value for college was a family inheritance for him. Gay, who is now a professional in his 40s, probably can't recall one classroom lesson that he learned in college but will never forget the day his father showed up on campus and how this act of caring got him back on track. His story illustrates that sometimes parents getting involved in a student's college experience is not an act of control, but rather an act of love. What he most remembers from college is that time when his father loved him enough to drive hundreds of miles just to talk to him about his grades. Undoubtedly his father felt pride not in having an athlete son, but having a *student* as a son; having a college graduate was more important. And so after remembering these stories, I later considered the importance of accounting for life after college—how professionals remember and appreciate their families and the impact their families have made on their education and careers.

The book is divided into four parts. Part I shares stories that are broadly focused on family. The second part shares a few stories on the role and impact of mothers. The third part is dedicated to fathers. And the book concludes with a broad focus on community from an international perspective. The final chapter offers a reflection on the entire text and implications for professional practice.

REFERENCES

Banks-Wallace, J. (2002). Talk that talk: Storytelling and analysis rooted in African-American oral tradition. *Qualitative Health Research, 12*(3), 410–426.

Du Bois, W. E. B. (1903). *The souls of Black folk.* Chicago: A. C. McClurg & Co. Retrieved February 10, 2011, from Bartleby.com/114/

Featherstone, J. (1989). Balm in gilead. *Harvard Educational Review, 59,* 367–378.

Smiley, T. (2006). *The covenant in action.* Carlsbad, CA: Smiley Books.

Part I
Family

1 It's a Family Affair
The Journey to College

Billy Brown and Breanna Brown

THE FATHER

Our parenthood journey began May 4, 1991. We were so excited to welcome our beautiful baby girl, Breanna, into our lives. I can remember my wife saying that she now understood a story her parents told her about her own arrival home. She recalled how her father would stand over her crib looking down at her saying, "I can't wait until she knows me!" We were now standing over our child thinking the exact same thing. Although we were certainly excited about all of the firsts that would come—rolling over, cooing, smiling, speaking words—what we really and truly anticipated the most was our child calling us " mom" or "dad" and understanding what that means.

As the months turned into years, and other firsts like the first day of kindergarten came, my wife and I realized that this journey wasn't going to be as long as we thought. It seems as if we went from changing diapers to packing lunch boxes in no time! Already, we were hearing declarations like, "I can walk to my class by myself!" It is truly amazing how children become independent so quickly. We welcomed that confidence, but we were also saddened by the idea that she might not need us as much as we thought she would. We never thought about how our desire to be supportive and nurturing parents might clash with her need to be a "big girl." However, the adolescent journey proved to be filled with many curves—bends in the road which our daughter would need help maneuvering. It was in those times that our parental roles were more clearly defined.

My wife quickly became the expert on friendship woes and the go-to person for school projects and field trips. When most kids secretly wanted their parents to be unavailable to chaperone, our daughter was confirming that mom would be attending the next school function. It was amazing to see how much she appreciated the value of having mom so close and involved. My wife's role remained relatively unchanged throughout high school. However, my role was becoming more defined and so was my bond with my daughter. As she became more interested and involved in sports, she began turning to me for guidance. It was amazing how we went from years of it not being cool to have dad so close to her proclaiming, "The game starts at 5:00. Can you come by 4:30 to help me warm up?" It was a special time for both of us as I watched her break school records and even compete on a state level. In fact, the time we spent together on the volleyball court and track, solidified a bond between us on a more personal level. Before long, she was asking my advice on careers and colleges. We would spend many evenings in my home office—she on one computer and me on another—searching colleges and discussing the pros and cons of our selections. My wife would make jokes about our spending so much time researching schools and their local areas. She said it was like we were going off to school together. Little did my wife know she was right. I wasn't fortunate enough to follow a traditional college path. My choice out of high school was to enlist in the U.S. Marine Corps. So, I didn't get to experience the college search. Although I would go on to attend college, I was relegated to attending whatever college was near the Marine base. So, being a part of my daughter's research period was truly exciting for me personally and as a father. All I could think about were the hours that my grandmother would spend working with me and telling me the stories of how she grew up and didn't have a chance to go to high school. Now, I was witnessing my own daughter having an experience that I didn't get to have. I was so proud of what a dedicated student she had been over the years and how her work ethic had now made available multiple college opportunities.

Eventually, the searches then turned into road trips to schools in Missouri, Georgia, and New York. These trips were exciting for the entire family including our 3-year-old, who was now asking, "When am I going to college?" The entire family was excited and ready to go for each trip. We all looked forward to touring the various campuses. I think the tours conjured different feelings in each of us. Our daughter was simply excited about the possibility of each new campus eventually becoming her new home. For my wife, it was a bit of a stroll down memory lane as she remembered her college days, and for our other two children I think it was a glimpse at what could be if they worked as hard as their sister. But, for me the campus visits were a reminder of how my daughter had changed my family's history.

We approached each college visit with deep excitement to have her entire family emerged in the experience, however, we started to see a discouraging trend among schools. No matter the size of the school, we would always hear the same type of speech during the informational meetings. It would start something like, "Once you arrive on campus, you'll become your own person. Your parents will have no access to any of your school records . . . unless you allow them." The student would be led off to learn about the wonderful experience of college and they would begin directing messages regarding financial aide and private loans to the parents! I remember walking away from the college visit thinking that I was nothing but a financial donor from this point on. It was really disheartening because all I could think about were the years that my wife had put into being such an involved classroom mom, the afternoons I spent coaching my daughter on the track field, and of course, the days and nights my daughter and I sat in my office scouring through the computer for hours researching schools. We were now being eliminated—not by our child but by the school.

Our relationship with our children is one where we teach them the importance of their decision making during the formative years so that they have solid decision-making foundations when they leave our home. We did not want to rob our daughter of her independence when she left for college. In fact, we felt very proud that she was well-prepared to leave home. She had shown herself to be honest, trustworthy, academically focused, and quite disciplined. All we were looking for was an opportunity to be a small part of the next 4 years—even if that simply meant being kept abreast of her productivity. My wife, in particular, had a really hard time understanding why we couldn't even receive copies of grades. In some way, we felt that our roles had been diminished to a signature on a check.

In the end, our daughter chose a school over 800 miles away from home, and we supported her decision without hesitation. Ultimately, it is about the school being the best fit for the student, and we felt that her choice was absolutely a perfect fit for her. We allowed her to spread her wings and encouraged her to work hard and to also enjoy her college years. Now a college junior, our daughter has done well and enjoys both her school and friends. We are so glad that we supported her decision to venture such a far distance from home. The only thing that I would change about the last 2.5 years would be policies established by the institution that forces engaged parents to be sideline observers. I would really like to see colleges include parents in every aspect of the orientation/student experience. It doesn't matter how much Internet research a parent does, or, how many college visits they attend, nothing can prepare a parent for the emotional moment of turning to leave a child in an unfamiliar environment.

Breanna has made her college experience a family matter. She makes it a point to remind us about family weekends. Her little brother, Jaden, has become a regular at these events. All of her college friends love for her to bring Jaden by to see them when he comes to visit. During one visit, Jaden was able to visit some of her classes as well as attend a hockey game. Our son so loves the trips that he talks about them for months afterwards. Breanna has even created a Skype account for him so they can have regular video calls, and he can continue to be a part of her college life. Her constant willingness to open her experiences to all of us has also created an excitement in her younger sister, a high school junior, about what lies ahead for her own future. As parents, seeing our other children inspired by Breanna's adventure is priceless . . . but also something that could not happen if our daughter wasn't willing to be open and inviting with her family.

Our daughter's actions indeed indicate that having her entire family involved in her college years is important to her. From inviting her aunt to attend a sleepover with some of her college friends, to including her grandmother, grandfather, and family friends in various video production class projects, Breanna continues to allow all of her family to be involved in her college experience. Her choices remind us that even though she wanted to leave home to attend school, she clearly still desires her family close.

THE DAUGHTER

Now a senior in college, Breanna Brown wrote the following statement as part of her application to graduate school . . . it seemed fitting to share it here as an illustration of how she appreciates her family's influence on her educational goals. She had not read her father's essay and he had not read hers, but yet they complement one another perfectly.

Telling Tales

Cave drawings, hieroglyphs, camp stories . . . every culture has had their way of telling tales. Storytelling has been an element of human culture since prehistoric time. In my own culture, storytelling was the last link my ancestors had to their native land of Africa, and through the generations my family has continued that tradition. In every generation of my family there has been a storyteller, a writer, or a creator. My great-grandfather Joseph Mobley was a man of many tales. Although I was never granted the chance to meet him, my mother would often tell me about how Grandpa Joe would tell exciting stories of our family's history that kept all the children and adults enthralled. After Grandpa Joe, the next storyteller was my Nanny (grandmother) Joyce. Even today Nanny writes love poems that sometimes turn themselves into song ballads. She has a favorite love poem that she wrote, and if asked about it she instantly bursts into song. Following in the footsteps of my grandmother came my Aunt Toby. My aunt is a writer of poems, scholastic articles, and books. She loves writing so much that she is working on a children's book just for fun. During holidays Toby would tell me bedtime stories of magnificent characters whose terrible actions always met with happier endings. Stories were always of great value to me even as a child. My father's job kept my family constantly on the move. I learned to love the character of people because I often came into contact with so many of them with each new move. I often studied people as if they were on stage. I began to see the world as a stage and people as very interesting players. It was difficult leaving a place after having barely arrived. So, books became my refuge. When I read, I would become the main character and the book was my world. I was the narrator. In middle school, my fascination with stories broadened to film, and that forever changed the way in which I viewed things. I began to realize that just like the generations before me, I also had a talent—a talent that could be used to create stories. But I moved this talent out of the home and off of the porch—my ambition was to create movies. Now I mark the start of a new generation and a new goal to entice, to enthrall, to spin tales, and to show an audience life in a way that they may have never seen it before.

Grabbing Goals

Raised in a military home, I was taught that, if I was going to do something, I needed to do everything and anything to achieve that goal—no matter how impossible others judged my odds. I missed my senior prom to look at colleges and chose to attend a school with one of the most unique electronic media programs in the country. My college choice was so different from my friends. Although my college is over 1,000 miles away from home, the majority of my classmates went to college in state. My father has consistently told me, "You go where you need to go; we will work things out once you are there." If ever there was a story to inspire me, to give me reason to diligently pursue writing and film, it would be my father's.

Born and raised in one of the most infamous projects in Atlanta, Georgia, my father grew up in an environment where almost no one thrived. Yet he soared. As a young man, he did everything he could to put himself in a positive environment. He joined the Boy Scouts, faked his address so that he could attend a school outside of his neighborhood, enrolled in the military, and ultimately escaped a world that few people ever manage to leave. After the military he earned a management position with Wachovia, and ever since that day he has received a promotion approximately every 2 years because of his persistent pursuit of his goals. From my father I learned dedication, diligence, and overcoming the negatives in life.

In my earlier years of grade school, one of my teachers described me as a child, "not able to learn at a quick pace." I was placed in remedial classes. At the request of my mother, the principal investigated the situation. Eventually it was my principal who discovered that there was never a problem with my ability to learn. Rather the problem was my vision—I required glasses. Surely enough, the glasses improved my focus in class. Since that experience, I have worked 10 times as hard in every aspect of my life to prove to that teacher that she was wrong about me. I know that she can no longer see me and that she has no way of knowing about my accomplishments, but I know that I am proving her wrong and that's enough for me. These experiences are what I rely on to ground my work. They push me to bring the best to my writing projects. They push me to be different.

Refocusing the Frame

In many of the books that I have read and movies that I have watched, the writers often create protagonists that the audience can easily understand. But, I seek to challenge the notion that a character must be paper-thin. Life is a complex process. Why shouldn't the movies that we watch capture that complexity? Too often the audience is able to guess the ending before the climax of the film. I want my movies to reflect the real twists and unexpected turns that come in life. If you were to visit my father's old neighborhood, you would never be able to envision that this now accomplished corporate executive grew up there. My father first taught me about surprise endings. I want to tell stories that cause you to truly think, to dig deep, and to investigate further in order to discover the root of the problem, as did my school principal. I do not aspire to create movies that simply satisfy. Instead, I aim to create worlds that provoke. There is a quote from Dziga Vertov that is written on the inside of many of my journals: "My road is towards the creation of a fresh perception of the world. Thus, I decipher in a new way the world unknown to you." My goal has perpetually been to captivate, to bring forth emotion, to make the audience try to peer around a corner because it's killing them to not know what is there. In order to achieve my goals, I have been exposing myself to as many different subjects and classes that I can. Art history, interactive narrative, game design, psychology, studio art, sculpture, poetry, short story, documentary production, geology, astrology, my list goes on. I speculate that education can never truly end for a writer, that there is no information that a writer need not know. A scientist does not need to possess knowledge of an artistic piece like Marcel Duchamp's "fountain," but a writer may have a character down the road that is a scientist. So, having a background in science is something that will be necessary in order to create a convincing character. This is why simply graduating with a bachelor's degree could never be enough for me. I desire to continue my education and further myself, until there is nowhere else to go.

2 Love Lessons From "The Hood"

Ashley Hazelwood

SAYING GOODBYE

Have you ever seen someone cry for 24 hours without end? My mother cried that entire Saturday. Of course, that sparked me to cry as well. The emotions were both bitter and sweet. The journey to college was marked with bitterness because I was required to move to Boston College months earlier than my counterparts. I was invited to attend a 6-week transitional summer program that would give me a so-called "leg up" over the other freshmen that would begin their college experience in the fall of 2004. I had literally just walked off the stage of my high school graduation, with no real time to celebrate. The excitement came as I thought about finally being able to leave my wretched hometown. This was a place where I felt misunderstood. It was a place in which I was the outlier, wrongly ascribed the identity of the "smart girl who thought she was better than everyone." My family environment often fell short of the haven I needed. But this was the place I knew intimately. It was home. Moments until my departure I experienced both the longing to leave and a pull to stay.

WHERE THE GRASS IS GREENER

Boston College was too perfect. I had never seen a place like this before. It took me quite a while to believe that my parents wouldn't one day show up and take me home. I felt like I was at a sleep-away camp! The grass (or fake grass) was neatly cut. There was no litter and the sunshine was bright up on Chestnut Hill. I was eager to learn about the Inbound and Outbound hoopla regarding the train (or the T) so I could go into downtown. Everything was everything . . . that is until everything really meant nothing at all. I was alone. My peers seemed to be preoccupied with meeting new people while I yearned to form lasting friendships. I wasn't originally the partying type but soon became one so that I would not fade into the background. I quickly found a Federal Work Study job on campus where I became a short order cook in the Dining Hall. I worked until well after midnight three times a week. I did all I could to be active, busy, and fully engaged in college. None of what I did, however, filled that unexplainable loneliness. Why was I here?

I first came to understand my position at Boston College when I was assigned a mentor through the Black Student Forum (BSF). First, I was unsure as to what BSF was and what they did. My mentor who was firm but gentle told me how important it was to build a support network with other Black students while at BC. She read me like an open book. "Girl, I know how you must be feeling! Lonely. Sometimes you want to go home. Well I'm here for you and all those feelings are NORMAL!" I did not know this girl but at that moment, I somewhat understood that my being at BC was bigger than me. There had to be other Black students who came before me and felt what I was feeling. I was standing courageously on the shoulders of those brave Black and Brown students. I felt an obligation to excel in order to pay homage to the legacy of those students.

That eagerness to succeed also resonated deeply because of my family. My family was counting on me! I was taking one for the team as they say. My visually impaired Latina-Caribbean grandmother could only dare to dream about going to college. My father had sacrificed a full-time soccer scholarship to be my father. My mother worked various jobs to build up a repertoire, making her fit to work as an administrator in New Jersey court systems. I understood my being the first one to go to college as a blessed indebtedness to my family back home. My education was in many ways a dedication to my two siblings who were 4 and 5 years old at that time, to my next door neighbors who hustled to pay the mortgage, to my church family who prayed intensely over me before my departure, and most importantly to myself. The grass may not be green where I am from, but I had been raised on an acre of love and it was now harvest time.

DIVERCITY

I thought I knew all about diversity before college. I attended a high school that accepted students based on a racial/ethnic quota. Twenty percent of every race flooded the hallways. I was certain that this experience prepared me for meeting new people at school. But something unexpected happened. I could not connect with White folks at Boston College. They were different. They weren't "cool as hell" like the other White students I had encountered back in Jersey City. I didn't get the "nod" that we all know in the city from these White people. In fact, many of them looked right through me—literally letting the door slam in my face. Even worse, there were Black students who were nothing like the Black people I knew! White or Black, many of the people on campus made me feel uncomfortable. The constant stares, generalizations about Black students in class, and the hyper-visible cliquing that occurred in the dining halls ignited a fire within me. Diversity in school seemed to be an empty word that was thrown around because it sounded nice. But the education that I received at home—from my family and my city—was filled with much more vitality and meaning!

At home, I knew diversity to mean a sincere love and embrace for others. I grew up in church and was always taught that everyone deserved respect regardless of who they were. In fact, my parents, both immigrants to this country, taught me these lessons after having been "othered" for most of their life. They told me stories about Americans, specifically African-Americans, accusing them of coming over to the states and taking their jobs. The challenge of creating community despite of perceived cultural differences was first observed on my block in Jersey City, not on a college campus. At home, I saw the differences between the various groups within the African Diaspora. Yet at the same time I saw the yearning among all of us to be identical. I knew very early that diversity was both intra-cultural and cross-cultural. My city taught me that. And culturally rich events were organically created right in my backyard. All of my friends could agree that my home was the place to be! Often, my mom would have big barbecue gatherings at my house and I was allowed to invite all of my friends. She cooked tons of food, played music, and we socialized until the streetlights came on. A deep respect and a genuine desire to come together in a world that screamed for us to tear each other apart was what connected all of the different people and cultures that populated my world as a teen. At home, learning about other cultures was an authentic endeavor. Everyone was looking to make that connection to another regardless of how different our households might have been. But this wasn't the case at college.

I found it hard to understand the hostility present at school. What had people of color done to the White community at Boston College to warrant so much tension? I could see right through the fake smiles. I noticed every time their eyes shifted from my face to the floor. I saw their looks when students of color had events in the quad. They didn't want to say hello and they didn't want to join. They looked at us funny even when we walked to class in a group, just like they did. Our campus was filled with things to do, but it was empty in spirit. No love was present.

It took me a few years to put all the pieces together. I learned about racial divides. I learned about social justice and systemic oppression. I learned that I was privileged to attend college but marginalized when perceived as a Black woman from the inner city. I learned about homelessness and poverty. I learned about Black people and White people, Latino people and Asian people. I felt compelled to attend different cultural events on campus. I was encouraged to say hello to students of color that I didn't know just to ensure that they felt welcomed. I worked as a counselor in the same program that brought me to Boston College. It brought me life to help students like me adjust to BC life. I knew how lonely it could be.

I'M HOME! BUT MY KEY'S JAMMED

During the first few holiday breaks, I felt awkward being home. I was uncomfortable having conversations about school with the people around me. At times, I wish I had been allowed to stay at school. Every condition, every person, every interaction was a philosophical struggle. Being at home again made me wonder about so much. I struggled to better understand the circumstances that were trapping some of my community members. I wondered about where Jersey City fell on the oppression spectrum. And I struggled to understand my position in the world. I found myself in a familiar place but an uncomfortable setting. While at college, I learned so much about the broad social challenges affecting my hometown. But surely, there was no one to talk to about my education once I returned home. Who would be interested? And why would they listen to me—I'd been gone and had become a distant relative to my own neighborhood.

God sent my pastor to be the first advocate. He sensed a rumbling in my spirit. I became angry and saddened by the conditions around me. I finally began to understand why my pregnant friends seemed to think I was better than them. I began to feel ashamed yet blessed by my upbringing. Even though my parents fought, they fought under the roof of a brownstone home with a garden in front. I had my own room and never went without anything—new shoes, new clothes, and all the latest technologies. My brother and sister were privileged too. They could count on me to help with homework when I was at home or call me on the phone when I was at school. My grandmother lived 5 minutes away and I had my own room at her house as well! I had my own car and was making good grades in school. In the grand scheme of life, I had it made. Coming home was a humbling experience for me, teaching me how to count my blessings.

Along the way, I realized that every single person around me was an advocate. But I had to be in a position where my heart could receive the special type of support, knowledge, and insight that people from my community could offer. Who was I to deem those around me lazy? The disgust I had once felt transformed into a deep compassion for the men, women, and children in my city. My eyes were wide open and I was going to keep them that way. I thought about how valuable the interactions were between my ex-boyfriends and me. As Black men growing up fatherless, I realized that they were trying to break the chain. They had authored their own definitions of manhood. Their approach to manhood might not have been perfect but it was a good effort. Someone should have told them that. My community had taught me things and I didn't even know it or appreciate it until that raw and authentic education was no longer present in my life. I thought about how vital affirmation was in my life and in the lives of those around me. I would undoubtedly need this affirmation when I returned back to BC after the holiday break. This time, I returned to campus with a whole set of different feelings and conclusions. First, I clearly saw my purpose and understood my responsibility. I loved my family and wanted their dreams to come alive in and through me. I also valued my home experiences even more after having been away at college. I could appreciate the fact that I learned the most about diversity while home in the city. In Jersey City it wasn't a term carelessly thrown around. Instead, it was demonstrated through the random acts of love we shared with each other. Finally, I returned with the knowledge that I was incredibly blessed. Everyday, thoughts of all that I don't have attempt to overshadow everything that I do have. It is a battle. While at BC, there were times when I was made to feel that I was nothing and had nothing to offer. But at home, I was made to feel that as a college student, I had everything—I was living the dream. I realized how important it was for me to return home. To return often and to stare intently at the circumstance. I know that the door is always open at home. My community is the entryway to my soul and the pathway to my future. Regardless of how far I go, I don't ever need to knock—they know me here. And so, that spring I confidently began the journey back to school with a healthy dose of home deep in my heart. As I closed my eyes and rested my head along the window of the $15 dollar Fung Wah bus from New York City to Boston, I pictured the faces of my family, neighbors, friends, and even distant ancestors quietly whispering, "hold on, keep going, hold on, press forward." And to this I said, "Amen," which means to acknowledge the spirit and presence of God that had been guiding me all along. Indeed, responsible for my success was the incredible spirit that made me and those beautiful spirits that raised me. And it would be those beautiful kindred spirits who would provide warmth when the climate on campus got too chilly. I pressed through my challenges to graduate from Boston College in May 2008. Since then, I have gone on to pursue other degrees in distant lands. But when it was all said and done, after completing my master's degree, I came home to use it. I now work as an educator at a college in New Jersey and I live in Jersey City, my hometown. It feels incredible to value my community, understand my community, and situate my professional career in my community. There truly is no place like home.

3 Home Training
Family, Struggle, Resilience, and Everything in Between

Anthony R. Keith, Jr.

A HUMBLE JOURNEY OF SUCCESS

For many, reaching the age of 30 is a major milestone. People often measure their lives by the marker of "30." What have you accomplished so far? What does the future hold? For me, "30" literally marked three decades of incredible life experiences. By the age of 30, I had already become a trailblazer in my family—already marking my path as the ancestor who did it differently. The list of accomplishments was long and the life experiences were deep. I was the first person in my family to earn both undergraduate and graduate degrees, to live in five different U.S. states, to travel to over 15 different countries, to work professionally as a university administrator, to teach college courses, to perform spoken word poetry on the lawn of the White House, and to dance with Archbishop Desmond Tutu on his 79th birthday. These had been 30 good years.

But when I reflect back on my life, I appreciate that these accomplishments were not the only things that have given my life meaning. I am also the son of a strong single-parent mother. I am the child of a successfully recovering drug- and alcohol-addicted father. I grew up in predominately Black, low-income communities in the politically motivated metropolis of Washington, DC, and Prince Georges County, Maryland. Violence, drug abuse, criminal activity, broken family structures, and poor performing schools systems were all socioeconomic fabrics of my neighborhoods.

I am a so-called poster child for Black boys who successfully "make it out of the hood"—which, for the record, is a concept I refute. Actually, I still struggle with sharing my school and professional experiences with my family without sounding pretentious. But I believe they understand my humility would never be usurped by narcissism. Whenever I return back to my old neighborhoods, my friends and extended family are excited to see me and want to hear about my most recent academic accomplishments. They always say, "Tony, I knew you would be the one who made it." I don't know what "it" is. I want to make it clear that I never "made it out of my community." Instead, I write this chapter as a person who continues to navigate "through my community," using education as my vehicle and humility as a compass. Therefore, in this chapter, I share memories about my community hoping to refocus educators' views of families and their values. Throughout this essay, I have weaved in excerpts from many of my original poems. Poetry is an additional tool of reflection and criticism that I often use to better understand my life experiences. By hearing my story, other educators might be able to see family not as an external institution, but rather as an additional site to fully understand the student experience.

FAMILY REUNIONS: LEARNING TO VALUE LOVE AND SOLIDARITY

We fear what we love
Being awesome is a monster inside closets
Watching us sleep, stealing our dreams in the dark
And when we wake, we forget
How amazing we could be
If we just turned the lights on
If we only pulled the cover from over our eyes
Placed our feet on the ground, and
Boldly proclaimed that WE ARE NOT AFRAID OF GREATNESS
No matter how many nights we spend shivering
Scared of our own success
We will at some point, get a full night's rest, and
We will rise with the sun
and like the sun, we will be bright and blinding and bold and hot
    and huge
and people will need us to survive the cold and the night

I used to attend family reunions. Every summer, generations of my maternal relatives would gather at Kenilworth Park in northeast Washington, DC. Some came from as far as South Carolina and others only had to take a few steps from their front porch, community block, or metro stop. My mom, my sister, and I would plan our quick trip the day before. We stuffed chicken, ribs, salads, sodas, and bottled water into small white styrofoam coolers. My sister and I always made sure we had our bags packed—complete with candy, playing cards, and bathing suits. We would synchronize our arrival time with my grandmother, aunts, and cousins the night before—just to ensure no one was left out on the big day. The night before each reunion felt like Christmas Eve and I barely slept because of the excitement. My sister and I woke up with the sun and drove my mother crazy by constantly asking, "When are we going to leave?"

The moment we climbed out of our car and set our gaze toward the gigantic pavilion where all of our family sat talking and laughing, we knew the reunion was here! We knew which babies we would hold first, which kids we would play with, and which elders to immediately hug. We knew whose hamburgers to eat and whose salads to avoid. We knew we had 45 minutes to play before the pool opened—which gave us just enough time to bribe our grandmother for money for the ice cream truck. We knew which family members had gin and tonic for breakfast and wouldn't hesitate to dance an inebriated, yet graceful, two-step when the DJ transitioned from hip hop to the oldies. I think we had the same DJ every year because his speakers always thumped family favorites like Chuck Brown's "Run Joe" or Little Benny's "Cat in the Hat" or Kool Moe Dee's "Do You Know What Time It Is?" The basketball courts and playgrounds were crowded with presumably the next NBA star, double-dutch rope contests, and my favorite— freeze tag! It never rained. We would stay all day and all night. My sister and I would pass out from fatigue on the car ride home with smiles on our faces—already prepared to share stories about the reunion over breakfast the next day.

I used to attend family reunions until I was about 12 years old, when a dispute between relatives turned tragic. I do not remember the full story, but I recall the presence of guns, loud displays of violent masculinity, my grandmother's frustrated brows, and the DJ's music coming to an abrupt silence. The reunion was over and everyone dispersed. I asked my mother on the ride home when was the next family reunion, and she said, "There won't be another one." My family reunion took place in Ward 5—which, at the time was one of DC's most underserved districts. According to a 2011 report by NeighborhoodInfo DC:

> Between the early 80's and late 90's, about 40% of the population in Ward 5 did not have high school diplomas, 10% were unemployed, 27% were living in poverty, 67% of households were headed by single mothers, and roughly 32% of violent crimes were reported in the area.

I never thought about the socioeconomic conditions surrounding the neighborhood in which my family gathered every year. I never cared to know why some of my male family members carried weapons in their pockets, or stashed guns in their cars. I did not think to ask my mother why police cars often circled through that neighborhood. I paid very little attention to the people living on the streets or why we were celebrating my cousin's release from prison. All I knew was the reunion was a rare occasion to see my family and enjoy their love and good spirits. I did not know my family was from the "hood" until violence peered its ugly head into our reunion. When violence, poverty, and crime disrupt the beautiful ethic of love and solidarity, the effects can be detrimental on any community. It can transform love into discontent and wage a gap between loved ones. Unfortunately, we have not had another reunion at Kenilworth Park. Many of my relatives moved out of Washington, DC and are now living in the predominately Black suburbs of Maryland. We are no longer neighbors in the same hood.

THE FAULTS OF A FATHER: LEARNING TO VALUE HUMILITY AND LOYALTY

> *no more dusty floors*
> *no more squeaky floors*
> *only whispers heard in the wind*
> *no more sadness*
> *wishful gladness*
> *no more because a new day will begin*
> *no more agonizing pain*
> *no more frozen rain*
> *only tears cried of joy*
> *no more frustration*
> *in any duration*
> *this man was once a boy*
> *It's all over*
> *the gloom that hovered*
> *nothing to do but smile*
> *smelling seashells*
> *pennies in wishing wells*
> *and ooohh stars how they fly*

I grew up in a family predominately of women. After my father left the household, my mother appointed me as the "Man of the House." I was charged with taking care of the "manly" chores—mostly taking out the trash and fixing things around the house, but I was also socialized to protect her and my sister. I made sure my sister and I were at school on time, and that I was the last person in the house to go to sleep. I learned how to cook and wash clothes by the time I was 8 years old. My social cues for male gender expression came from other male friends, their fathers and a few extended family members on my dad's side. I was a short, skinny, late bloomer—whose voice did not have an inkling of baritone until I graduated from high school. I exhibited behaviors mostly attributed to women and became accustomed to fielding questions about my sexuality. Being called "gay," "faggot," and "sissy" were quite common for me. I usually denied the accusations or reacted in violence to protect my immature and wounded sense of self.

In fact, violence and aggression were the only ways I knew how to express my masculinity. I was modeling the behavior of the few male family figures with whom I had frequent interaction. Unfortunately, those interactions were not always positive. I remember seeing violent masculinity transposed for passion, after visiting with a female cousin who was beaten deaf in one ear by her husband while she slept. I remember my mother hurling wire hangers at my father after he snatched jewelry off her neck. My oldest male cousin has been in several fights, survived multiple gunshot wounds, and I once visited him and my uncle in prison, in the same year. I remember punching this White kid in the face on the bus ride home from school because he said he was not afraid of me. I once launched multiple blows at another guy's head on the playground after he teased me for being short and skinny. I shoved a boy into the chalkboard at school because he made a joke about my mother. Once, I even gave a kid a black eye and stomped on his face after he told other people in my neighborhood that he could "whoop my ass."

I would even fight my sister—punching and kicking her in the most violent display of sibling rivalry. Yes, I even fought girls. I cared very little about gender differences when it came to violence. I also resisted any form of authority. If reprimanded by a teacher, I reacted with sharp language laced with profanity. Most of the teachers were older White women who I thought were senile jerks. Once, I told a high school teacher to "shut up and fuck off!" I often felt like some of my teachers were afraid to teach me and the other Black boys in the class because of our behavior. I did not always have "success" in fights. I suffered bloody noses, hurt feelings, and public embarrassment on school playgrounds and cafeterias. At that time, it was a badge of honor.

Although I was steadfast on becoming a juvenile delinquent, my father was committed to recovering from his disease of addiction and reconnecting with my sister and me. I know it was not easy for him. By the time I was a teenager, my father had lost his job, his home, his second marriage, and was mourning the death of his father and his sister. Finally, he succumbed to the weight of it of his own free will and entered a drug rehabilitation program. My mother once took my sister and me to visit and I remember seeing resilience and strength in his eyes. He was going to get through this. It was awkward to listen to him recount tales of evading drug dealers and smoking crack cocaine with other close family members and friends. This was not my father. This was not the man who would whisper secrets in my and my sister's ears when we were infants. This was not the man who nick-named me "Skin head" and "Shawty Bus Stop." This was not the man who would catch crickets with his bare hands or help my sister and me collect lightening bugs. Perhaps my inability to recognize him as my father made his absence easy to deal with.

Around my sophomore year of high school I received a phone call from my father informing me he was "clean" and wanted to rebuild our relationship. I explained how difficult life had been without him. I shared stories of being picked on and bullied by other boys who thought I was "soft" and how I yearned for father figures like the ones my friends had. He listened without interruption and said, "Thank you my son, I needed to hear those things." I did not know that he, too, was wounded. I forgave him. That conversation was cathartic and necessary for the healing process to begin. Over the last few years "Pop" and I have developed a bond that is solely based on unconditional love and support for one another. He is on the ministerial staff of his church, remarried to a wonderful wife, owns his home, has countless degrees and certificates in counseling, is committed to sobriety, and he is undoubtedly my best friend. He is a dynamic speaker, preacher, and mentor with a gift for using humor and inspiring words to positively affect the lives of others. He has substituted an addiction to drugs with an addiction to loving himself more and following the path of God. The best thing about Pop is how comfortable he is with showing emotion and affection both physically and verbally. In addition to kissing me on my forehead when I see him, he regularly sends me empowering text messages and e-mails. Here are a few of my favorites:

> I know you may not need what I'm sending, but ain't a damn thing you can do about it!

> No matter what it looks like now~ eyes have not seen, ears have not heard, and neither has it entered into the heart of man what God has in store for you.

> You're a good man, you're a great man, you're an intelligent man, you are a learned man, you are a man with vision, you're a man worth far more than your weight in silver & gold. Great things await your arrival. Remember delay is not .. . . . .denial!

> My subject for Good Friday is "persecuted for a purpose." let that marinate with you for a minute . . . holla ~Pop

Those messages reinforce and strengthen my masculinity and make me believe my father is a true artist of words. He makes me a better poet.

A MOTHER'S LOVE: LEARNING TO VALUE LEADERSHIP AND INCLUSION

> *Sometimes, my mom would say:*
> *"you gotta break your legs to recognize how far your arms can
>   reach"*
> *Sometimes, my mom would say:*
> *"you gotta plug your ears to recognize how far you can see"*
> *Sometimes, my mom would say:*
> *"you gotta give up what you want to recognize what it is you really
>   need"*

My mother was instrumental in helping me develop not only a healthy masculinity but also an unconscious feminist identity. She often worked late nights, came home exhausted, and fell asleep fully dressed with her eyeglasses still on her face. I would go into her room before bed and turn off her TV, take off her eyeglasses, and kiss her goodnight. It was always a joke the next morning that her son "tucked her in." But, I felt like it was my domestic duty to ensure that the women of my household were safe at all times. So, I have always chosen to ascribe to a more "protective" role in my relationships with women. Some might argue it makes me a sexist, but I never felt I needed to exert power over girls or women for self-gain. If anything, I wanted to ensure the women in my life were valued and included. According to author David Ikard's book, *Breaking the Silence: Toward a Black Male Feminist Criticism* (2007), most Black men attribute the development of a feminist identity through an evaluation of the power dynamics within their personal relationships with Black women.

My mother also taught me about leadership and survival. She is a superhero. Mom would battle my father in court cases over custody and child support, and simultaneously work two jobs to keep us fed, clothed, and in a safe home. She relied on the neighborhood community for support and often had other single-parent mothers monitor my sister and me while she was away. I remember smoking a cigarette with one of my friends, in what I thought was a very private location in our apartment complex. Hours later, my mother came home and asked to smell my breath, lectured me about smoking, and grounded me for a week. On another occasion, my sister and I snuck out of the house late at night to play with some friends and within an hour my mom was at the playground in her pajamas with a belt in her hand eager to discipline us in front of our friends . . . and she did. I was convinced she had supernatural senses that could detect anything my sister and I did within a 100 miles radius. But actually, she was demonstrating leadership by utilizing the resources of the community to make a positive impact on those she loved the most—her children.

My mom also sacrificed time and money to ensure our survival. I remember my mother writing checks at the grocery store, knowing they would bounce, but it was a guaranteed way to get us food. We were probably eligible for food stamps but my mother chose to write "hot checks" instead. Perhaps it was her way of denying the realities of being a single mother of two children and living on a low income. Sometimes she even managed to "rob Peter to pay Paul" so that my sister and I felt special (not poor). One day my mom came home with boxes of designer sneakers for us; we were ecstatic because it was rare that she came home with anything beyond second-hand clothing or off-brand items. In retrospect, I never saw my mom buy anything for herself. After the divorce, she pawned her wedding ring and used the money to saturate our Christmas tree with presents. I remember feeling extremely loved and special that day. It was during those extraordinary moments that I realized my mother was teaching me to discern what a community needs and what a community wants. I started my first job at age 15 with the idea that my mother would never have to buy me anything I did not need. I took care of buying my own clothes, shoes, haircuts, and entertainment. I even gave her money sometimes when she asked, or if I felt like the family was in need.

Additionally, my mother also made sure every member of the community was valued and appreciated. She often took in "strays"—providing food and shelter for many of my sister's friends who were experiencing homelessness or having problems with their parents. My mom never complained about having another mouth to feed or finding space for another child to sleep in her home. Recognizing that everyone has potential and deserves to be loved and cared for has been one of the most important leadership values I learned from my mother. I think one of the major reasons I ended up in a career working for the social good is because she taught me principles of inclusion.

FROM KINDERGARTEN TO COLLEGE: LEARNING TO VALUE ACADEMIC SUCCESS

I have always been academically successful. I was in the Talented and Gifted (TAG) program and earned mostly A's and B's every reporting period from Kindergarten through 12th grade. I earned academic awards for writing and often served as a Master of Ceremonies for several school programs. In fact, my late grandfather used to call me "Mr. Guest Speaker." He was convinced I was a sharp wordsmith of sorts—as if he knew I was destined to be a poet. My father would often tell me that I'm from planet Pluto—not that I was an alien, but that for some reason I was always able to rebel against my socioeconomic conditions by excelling in education. hooks (2004) suggests any Black male seeking to move from bondage to freedom looks to education as a way out. That's exactly what I did.

Although I would still occasionally get into fights at school, I learned how to balance my gender performance with my academic performance. I was okay with being a "nerd" as long as I was able to keep my street credibility. Again, hooks (2004) explains that well-educated Black men have learned to act as if they know nothing in a world where a smart Black man risks punishment. It was important for me to sustain an authentic community membership and simultaneously excel as a scholar. I hoped that my academic success would become a part of my family and community's value system. Parents of friends would often tell my mom that they wished their children were "like Tony." The positive reinforcements from members of my community served as motivation to achieve academic excellence and more importantly sparked a cultural shift in how we valued education. Once I realized my educational accolades positively affected my family, I sought that same response from teachers as well. I

stopped rebelling against their authority, began to embrace their pedagogy, and thrived on their praises.

Therefore, choosing to become my family's first college graduate was an
easy decision. I was not a member of any college readiness programs. I did
not research the top academic programs or institutional rankings. I chose
to apply to the university that all of my friends were planning to attend.
The only requirement was that it not be too far from home. I completed my
college applications on my own. When I received the acceptance letter my
family was ecstatic! Although no one really knew what to do about financial
aid, registering for classes, or how to acquire textbooks, they knew I had the
capacity to figure it all out. My mother—for whatever reason—did not take
me to college. Instead, my father and my stepmother dropped me off at my
residence hall, helped me unpack, bought me some groceries, and left. I did
not have any other family members come visit my entire first year of college.

I wondered sometimes if they assumed everything was fine because I was
always a very independent child, or, if they did not visit because the environment was unfamiliar for them. I questioned if they would feel like they
belonged on a college campus. They never participated during sports events
or Parent and Family Weekends. I went home and called often. My mom
was always excited to hear from me. She never asked about my grades,
what I was learning in my classes, or what my future plans were after graduation. She was just glad to know her "baby" was ok. My grandmother
would occasionally put money into my bank account every few weeks, but I
largely relied on financial aid refunds and credit cards to pay for my education and living expenses.

During my first few years of undergrad I realized that my formative
schooling did not prepare me for the academic rigor of a university education. Perhaps, I was just an anomaly in the poor performing DC Metro
school system where expectations for minority student success are low. I
questioned whether I was intellectually capable of surviving in the college
environment. By the end of the year, I did not feel like I had the support of
my family anymore, and to make it worse, I was failing college. I strongly
considered withdrawing from the university with no intent to return. After
succumbing to two consecutive semesters of poor academic performance, I
sucked up my pride and went to the University Learning Center. Not only
did they provide me with tools for academic success, they referred me to
other campus departments and organizations that would aid in my journey to excellence. After joining several student organizations, participating
with the campus Cultural Center, and receiving mentoring from faculty
and staff, I formed a campus family that resembled my real family. I had
professors and administrators I deemed as aunts and uncles, and students I
referred to as siblings and cousins. My grades drastically improved.

The day I graduated from college was monumental. I had over 40 relatives in attendance. I distinctly remember my mother, with tears in her eyes,
breaking through the line of graduates to hug me as we entered the arena.

When I walked across the stage, my parents looked at each other—proud that despite everything the family had been through, their son was able to earn the family's first college degree. I decorated my cap with the phrase "The First, Not The Last," and allowed all of the young children in the family to wear it—signifying that they too can earn a college degree if they wish. Since then, my mother, father, two of my cousins, and my sister have earned post-secondary degrees!

ADDING FAMILY AND COMMUNITY TO THE EQUATION

My life tells the story of a little Black boy who, despite the odds, has been able to achieve success by integrating community and family values in educational endeavors. These values include: love, solidarity, humility, loyalty, leadership, inclusion, and academic success. Collectively these values can not only shape students' perceptions of their intellectual capacity, but also dictate their level of interaction within the educational environment. College students who share my story are likely to persist despite academic or social challenges because struggle is a part of their drive for success. These students are empowered during tough moments and will either seek out, or create, a network of resources to achieve their goals. For me, it was a Learning Assistance Center and my campus's Cultural Center, along with and supportive students, staff, and faculty of color.

Also, students who struggle are likely to recognize other students experiencing similar challenges and can be instrumental in developing coalitions of support. Although they may not serve as academic experts, they are life experts with cultural knowledge shaped by their communities. They know what it is like to feel excluded or not have access to supportive resources and thus the need to be creative and resourceful is an innate gift. For example, my mother instilled the value of inclusion and equity through her leadership and authentic care for the well-being of those in need. She indirectly taught me about power dynamics that exist between men and women and how gender performances are negotiated. Discovering that the majority of the students in my school were on free or reduced lunch, and most came from single parent homes, truly heightened my awareness of oppression and injustice within communities.

When a student values solidarity they can make a direct impact on the rate of college retention. Actively participating in family-like structures, full of authentic love and care, can foster a student's sense of loyalty to the mission and vision of any community—especially college campuses. I learned that from my "Pop." He yearned to mend a broken-family structure after his absence, and by communicating his desire and vision for a healthy father–son relationship we have become best friends. He and I are loyal to each other and recognize our interdependence. We often use the phrase "I'm okay, as long as you're okay." Although not all college students will share my story, they will enter the college environment with a set of value systems shaped by their own families and communities. It is those values that will determine the likelihood of success for both the student and the institution.

> *One day we will tip toe down hallways*
> *making footprints sound like earthquakes*
> *and we will awaken all those who are sleeping*
> *all those afraid to be acknowledged for daring to be different*
> *for those who hush, then they should command*
> *for those who run when they should stand*
> *for those who need to realize you cannot hide in the light*
> *it sticks to you like brown on Black skin*
> *like sap from trees, rooted in sweet soil*
> *you need to see that you are a star*
> *I literally see you in the sky*
> *Defying laws of space, time and gravity*
> *But humans are not supposed to be able to fly*
> *But you glide like the first leaf in autumn*
> *Your silhouette struts in daylight and dances with the moon*
> *You are part of a collective*
> *A critical mass of intellectuals governed by divine knowledge*
> *You are meant to be here with purpose*
> *Just like I am meant to be here with purpose*
> *We are purposefully meant to be here*
> *So the sick can become a healer*
> *The timid can become a leader*
> *The bully can become a teacher*
> *And the boogey man can become a poet.*

REFERENCES

hooks, b. (2004). *We real cool: Black men and masculinity.* New York: Routledge.

Ikard, D. (2007). *Breaking the silence: Toward a black male feminist criticism.* Louisiana: Louisiana State University Press.

Knight, M. G., Norton, N. E., Bentley, C. C., & Dixon, I. R. (2004). The power of black and latina/o counterstories: Urban families and college-going processes. *Anthropology & Education Quarterly, 35*(1), 99–120.

NeighborhoodInfo DC. (n.d.). DC ward profile. Retrieved September 30, 2011, from http://www.neighborhoodinfodc.org/wards/nbr_prof_wrd5.html

4 Speaking Those Things That Be Not as Though They Are

The Role of Faith in Caregivers' Educational Hopes for Their Differently-Abled Son

Michael D. Hannon and LaChan V. Hannon

A GROUNDING FAITH

In a world where absolute truths are as invisible as a broken heart, there is one thing we do know about parenting: The most valuable lessons we've learned about how devoutly and patiently God loves us, we've learned from being parents; the most valuable lessons we've learned about how unconditionally we're supposed to love God, we've learned from being parents of a child with autism. On any given day for our family of four, autism can represent the warring opposition between structure and flexibility, fact and reality, abstract and concrete, pretense and truth. But, at the center of it all, faith in what the Biblical apostle Paul has already spoken is our only resolve. In Philippians' first chapter (*Blue Letter Bible*, 1996–2012), he wrote, "And I am certain that God, who began the good work within you, will continue his work until it is finally finished on the day when Christ Jesus returns."

Someone once said to us, "When you meet one child with autism, you meet ONE child with autism." Autism looks vastly different from child to child, sibling to sibling, family to family. The variety in symptoms can be equally fascinating and frustrating. One minute can mean being docile and gentle or it can mean being furiously raging. It can be exhibiting confidence in the correct answer or expressing deep anxiety about even sharing at all. An autistic child can be hurt by being left out or be the lone leader with everyone following. Autism presents its own unique set of challenges and rewards and, consequently, has the potential to both cripple and strengthen one's belief systems—about relationships, faith, and education—at the same time.

AUTISM SPECTRUM DISORDER: WHAT IS IT AND WHAT DOES IT LOOK LIKE IN OUR FAMILY?

Our son, Avery, was diagnosed with Pervasive Developmental Disorder-Not Otherwise Specified (PDD-NOS) in January 2006. PDD-NOS is a specific condition within the broader diagnosis of the Autism Spectrum

Disorders (ASD). It is a developmental disability that the fourth edition of the *Diagnostic Statistical Manual of Mental Disorders—Text Revised* (DSM-IV–TR, American Psychiatric Association, 2000) defines as, "the presence of markedly abnormal or impaired development in social inter-action and communication and a markedly restricted repertoire of activity and interests" (p. 70). Our way of accepting and communicating that to our family, friends, and anyone else bold enough to ask, is simply acknowledging Avery has *a different way of thinking, seeing, listening, and responding.* As we first began to consult with specialists and access community resources about our concerns for Avery, we were never truly prepared for our meeting with the developmental pediatrician. Prior to this meeting, we sought the advice of our children's general pediatrician, specialists within our county's Early Intervention (EI) system, and an audiologist, among others. After spending time with Avery and consid-ering his presenting symptoms, the EI specialists tried to very delicately tell us. With a little nudging and a few pointed questions from LaChan, the EI providers hesitantly responded, "We are not qualified to make a diagnosis, but we will not be surprised if you hear the word 'autism.'" The evidence was sobering. Avery had very few words, exhibited very repetitive behaviors, and habitually rolled his wrists and ankles in the same way you might see gymnasts warm up their joints. Among other peculiar behavioral tendencies was his ability to stand and stare for hours on end. We will never know if those frequent episodes were seizures, and honestly speaking, a part of us does not want to know. But surely, we had not observed these behaviors in his older sister Nile's development.

WHAT HAPPENS BETWEEN NOW AND THEN? A K–16 PERSPECTIVE

We attribute whatever success our family has experienced with raising a child with autism to our faith in Jesus Christ and how that faith has enabled us to be competent and thoughtful parents and educators. As parents (of children with or without disabilities), we all participate in some form of vision casting for our kids. We thoughtfully consider how they learn best; the type of peers with whom they should connect in order to bring out the best in them; and the range of experiences and opportuni-ties we can offer to maximize their intellectual, emotional, spiritual, and academic development. However, we must admit that, at times, our vision for our children is grounded in our own selfish desires. We spend the early developmental years through adolescence attempting to construct an experience for them in which they move toward becoming responsible young adults. What happens, then, when it's time for your son or daugh-ter to leave home to pursue a post-secondary education? And to add a bit of complexity, what happens if s/he has a developmental disability, like an autism spectrum disorder? That's the conversation that has and will continue to take place in our house.

Colleges and universities have long abandoned the early philosophy of *en loco parentis* (in place of the parents) in an effort to encourage personal and academic responsibility in their students. The Family Educational Rights and Privacy Act (FERPA) actualizes this position, as institutions and families navigate the fine line of honoring a college student's rights while acknowledging that parents and caregivers naturally feel entitled to their students' educational portfolio. For parents of children with disabilities, navigating this process can become increasingly complex and potentially frustrating. The institutional characteristics we might consider for our "typically developing child" will not likely be the same for our son with autism spectrum disorder. Thankfully, we have never desired for any of Avery's educational institutions to act "in our place." Instead, we hope to nurture Avery's ability to find his own voice and advocate for himself when necessary. But, we also want him to remember his collectivist family values: values that responsibly include, engage, and consider our larger family network in decision making. And why would he abandon those values? From the time Avery enrolled in school at 3 years old, identified as a *preschool disabled student*, we have been intentionally and entirely engaged with his school personnel to develop, execute, and modify his Individualized Education Plan (IEP). We have gone so far as to take one district to due process to justify an appropriate summer educational placement (and we won!). Accessing services for students with disabilities in college, however, is quite different than in elementary and secondary education. Thankfully, practitioners and scholars are helping parents like us navigate this process while colleges work to effectively implement disability services in their respective institutions. Like many parents and caretakers of racially under-represented students, this presents quite a shift in philosophy. We work hard to raise our children to be accountable and transparent for close to 20 years (and in many cases more) before they leave for college. And, in the blink of an eye, they are encouraged to abandon such values under the guise of a socially constructed "adulthood," which requires a different type of accountability. We commit to remaining engaged in Avery's educational pursuits while Avery develops his own voice in order to advocate for himself. However, our convictions will not allow us to forsake our identity as his first team of advocates.

As parents and career educators, we know that more students with disabilities are enrolling in college than ever before. The HEATH Resource Center (1999) reported that the proportion of college freshman with disabilities nearly tripled between 1978 and 1998. As legislation such as the Americans with Disabilities Act of 1990 and Section 504 of the Rehabilitation Act of 1974 articulates the rights of students with disabilities on campuses, colleges are having to broaden the scope of services and accommodations to meet this population's collective needs. But, how do we (parents) prepare and position our children with disabilities for success, acknowledging the varying degrees of compliance found at post-secondary institutions?

Toward this end, Grigal and Hart (2010) co-authored an edited volume on post-secondary options for students with intellectual disabilities. Shaw, Madaus, and Dukes (2010) offer an equally valuable, comprehensive resource in helping both educators and caregivers prepare to transition their students with disabilities into college with suggestions on how to find an appropriate college placement, determining eligibility for disability services, and increasing self-determination in students. Scholarship within rehabilitation counseling, disability studies, and special education (among others) is highlighting how parents and institutions can work together to facilitate the success of students with disabilities in college. Although significant progress has been made since the passing of ADA, students with disabilities and their parents would likely report there is still much work to be done. Some of the scholarship appropriately discusses the challenges of increasing knowledge and understanding across entire college and university systems to better meet the needs of students with disabilities, particularly among faculty. Cook, Rumrill, and Tankersley (2009) found in a study of 307 faculty members in an 8-campus university system in the midwest that participants believed accommodation policies and disability etiquette were highly important and were being satisfactorily addressed within their institutions. Unfortunately, they also found that issues related to law, Universal Design for Instruction, and disability characteristics, although considered important, were not being adequately addressed and issues related to the provision of accommodations were either not considered highly important or weren't being addressed at all. It is quite scary and humbling to realize that the way we engage Avery's teachers now will not be the way we potentially engage with administrators in his college of choice. Allow us to share how this wonderfully unique experience has shaped both our personal and career identities.

WHAT DID THIS MEAN FOR US?

As we grieved the news of Avery's diagnosis, we were reminded of the scripture in Isaiah 53:5 (*Blue Letter Bible*, 1996–2012) that reads, "But he was pierced for our rebellion, crushed for our sins. He was beaten so we could be whole. He was whipped so we could be healed." We believed (and still believe) that Avery can be healed of all symptoms and challenges associated with his diagnosis. However, we are not so naive to think that we do not have an enormous responsibility to provide him with the most effective therapeutic and educational supports we can afford. The Bible tells readers in James 2, "that faith without works is dead" (*Blue Letter Bible*, 1996–2012). So, it has always been critical for us to be seekers of services, while relying on our professional and spiritual instincts to dictate what is most

helpful for Avery and his educational trajectory. Social science and education researchers have documented how mothers and fathers respond to this
experience differently. Here are our individual and collective narratives.

LaChan: Veteran High School English Teacher, Educational Advocate/Entrepreneur, and Behavior Specialist

I have not always identified myself as an educator. I began my first teaching
position when I was already 7 months pregnant with Avery, who is now
only 8 years old. So, at that time I could barely call myself a teacher. As
Avery developed and we explored the possibilities of what could be wrong,
teaching became more than just a job. It became a lifestyle. We were at a
crucial time in his development. Many would refer to this time as the "window of opportunity" of early intervention. I had but a moment to reach in
and pull out my son. Teaching was a large part of that. I learned from the
teachers, behaviorists, and therapists and did my best to apply that learning
in my home.

Home became the classroom. Every toy, every object was therapeutic
to the point that it wasn't until recently my children knew that there were
toys made "just for fun." Every interaction was an opportunity for Avery
to learn some new skill and for me to learn something about him. The
stakes were too high for anything to be done that was not a deliberate
attempt to produce the desired outcome. The art of differentiated instruction I learned from Avery. The creative ways to use anything as a multi-
function therapeutic tool I learned from Avery. How to respect and use a
student's learning preferences, I learned from Avery. How to negotiate a
power struggle between a teacher and student I learned from Avery. My
experience as a mother was professionally developing me as a classroom
teacher. Unlike some teachers, I did not have the opportunity to take my
teacher hat off at the end of the school day and replace it with my mom/
wife/sister/daughter hat. I came home from school and kept on teaching my
son. The idea of teaching to standards that was demanded by my school
was not a new idea, because anything less at home was not negotiable. My
classroom experience was perpetual. Lesson planning never ended. I was
becoming an educator. As a professional, I liken it to No Child Left Behind
(NCLB) and thoughts on high-stakes testing. With my students at school,
I know that I cannot control many of the variables and vulnerabilities presented in my classroom, but I can control myself and the energy with which
I make teaching and learning a priority for my students. I also learned this
from Avery. I chuckle to myself now when I hear someone say the words
"best practice" because that means absolutely nothing to Avery and any
other child with autism I have met. "Best practice" is only as relevant as its
current success.

You would think that a classroom of 25 students of varying abilities and
opinions would demand best practices from a teacher, but they did not;

they accepted what I gave them. For my child with autism, yesterday's success was a distant memory. After 2 months of noncompliance, tantrums, screaming, lateness, and tears from the both of us, I celebrated and was truly embarrassed the day I discovered how to turn the reprehensible task of asking nonverbal Avery to get dressed every morning into an interaction of relationship.

Me: *(teary eyed and pleading) Please Avery can we please just get dressed? I'm going to be late for work again.*
Avery: *(teary eyed) uuuugggg . . .*
Me: *We have to go downstairs and eat breakfast. Why won't you just let me put your clothes on? I don't have time to argue with you and do nothing. We have to go.*
Avery: *(tears and screams)*
Me: *(resigned) I give up. I don't know what you want me to do. Fine, Avery we will sit here and do nothing.*

Thirty seconds of silence and calm go by. As I'm sitting on the floor, Avery walks over, sits in my lap, and says "uuuugggg." He hugs me. I hug him back. He's not mad at me anymore, he just wanted to be hugged, squeezed, and loved on, not rushed through the morning without being acknowledged. That stung . . . DEEPLY. He taught me to listen with my eyes. His needs demanded I do something differently. And that I could control.

As I watched Avery grow and develop, it was important for me to surround him and myself with other educators who modeled that same level of commitment to their students. Those professionals had to understand strength-based instruction, practice learning from others, and embrace a truly student-centered approach to teaching and learning. It is because of my experiences with Avery that I understand it is not enough just to be a teacher and hope that students learned. Teaching has to be accompanied by learning on the part of the teacher. It has been the humble, flexible, and dedicated teachers that have had the most impact on Avery and his success. Unfortunately, although Avery is still in elementary school, some of his teachers and support staff have not embraced this same philosophy of teaching and learning.

For an entire year of my life, every single prayer I offered I did for Avery. And what God shared with me during that time was that Avery's needs would always be supplied. It took a long time for me to really understand that. I was very protective of Avery and wary of the people I allowed to influence him. We came across people who did not understand the intentionality of our decisions for Avery because we do everything purposefully. As his mother, I am charged with being his biggest advocate. As an educator and teacher, I know Avery's strengths. And, my philosophy has always been "use the strengths to supplement the weaknesses." I continually try to impress upon his teachers and specialists this philosophy. Some were on board and some were not. I encourage them to push Avery's areas of strength, even if that means creating a bigger divide between him and his classmates. When he was in Kindergarten, he was reading at a second grade reading level. I could have let teachers leave him in an age-appropriate setting, but why should I? There are so many areas where he struggles, why not allow him to excel in one area so that when the work does get harder he can remember that confidence. To not acknowledge his weaknesses is, quite honestly, denial, and would do Avery a great disservice. In my experience, many people strive for normalcy. Normal becomes the reference for appropriate development.

Question to teacher: "How is Avery doing during math?"
Answer from teacher: "Well compared to his peers he is doing well."
Comment to teacher: "I really do not have a baseline for other students so let me rephrase. How is Avery doing in relation to the expectations we have of him and his full capabilities?"

It is this desire and quest for normalcy that has caused me to challenge the beliefs I have as an educator and how I define normal for both of my children. Over the years, I have had to reevaluate the concept of fair versus equal and revise my expectations. Having taught both typically developing and special needs students, I have learned that every student cannot and should not be treated equally. Additionally, what is normal for one student, one family, is certainly not normal for another student, another family. Having a child with autism has opened up more possibilities of who he can become. It is so easy to assume that typically developing children will follow the rules, get good grades, and go to college. That is normal. That is what we expect. For right or wrong, we acknowledge their gifts and talents, and we cultivate them so long as those gifts and talents sit tandem to the academic aspirations we have for them. But a child with special needs, the child with autism, is allowed exceptions.

We, as parents, spent so much energy using his strengths to supplement his weaknesses that we have allowed for the possibilities. We have allowed for the opportunity of something other than college. I can remember being so happy the day Avery developed an interest in music. We bought every musical instrument we could. I rationalized my latitude by saying Avery was practicing self-expression, played to his preferences, and made exceptions to the "rules." But what I was really doing was allowing his personality to shine rather than the expectations I have of him to cast a shadow. Somehow, his disability facilitated a flexibility in my thinking—a flexibility that unfortunately my typically-developing daughter is not always afforded. Nile is a creative, sensitive, compassionate child who arguably has more love for the arts than Avery. Yet somehow, I am often desensitized to her great qualities and attributes because of MY will for her life and not God's will for her life. The idea of her not following a certain educational path so she can pursue her artistic dreams is a hard pill for me to swallow because she has the potential to be anything she wants to be. Or, maybe I should more honestly say, "anything I want her to be." I am slowly realizing how unfair it is that because of her consistent flexibility and enormous potential, I can potentially restrict her truest and most sincere expression. I am sometimes intrigued by the word choice of "typically-developing" that we educators often use to describe "normal" children. What exactly does that mean? Does it mean that this child will develop to be as typical as everyone else? If so, does that mean the special needs child is allowed to then be special?

Michael: Counselor and College Adviser

I had no idea how to make sense of Avery's diagnosis when I first heard it. I remember going home and crying. I remember calling my younger sister, Lia, to relay the message about how Avery's developmental assessment at 21 months matched the functioning level of a 6-month-old in some areas. As I began to acknowledge how my father–son relationship expectations might need to change, I was transitioning out of my job as a high school counselor to a new role as the counselor for a college access program for low-income, high potential high school students. For this unique program, I was hired to be the "college access expert." My job was to guide our students and their caretakers through the college transition process—from high school course selection and PSATs to first-year college transition and beyond. Naturally, as I engaged in this work and developed my sophistication in the small but highly nuanced college access world, the parallel process questions began to emerge: "Will Avery ever go to college?" "Will the professional work that is defining me now ever benefit my children, especially my son?" If I am totally transparent, there have been several times when I have been doubtful, which comes with a huge sense of guilt.

This is a bit ironic. . . . The wild irony in all of this is that my professional experiences as an educator have included work with students in both high school and college, many of those students fitting some criteria of vulnerable. In higher education, I worked in student affairs for 5 years, specifically in student leadership development and multicultural affairs on predominantly white campuses. I have been privileged to work with and support exceptionally talented college students of color with vision and maturity beyond their years. Many have confronted the challenges associated with being the first in their families to enroll and matriculate through college, which can be an emotionally and academically distancing experience. It requires them to appropriately engage with the academic and social challenges of college while attempting to maintain a healthy connection to their home communities. The high school students I've advised and counseled are overcoming obstacles that include being wards of the court or coming from families whose annual income barely exceeds $8,000. They have been victims (and survivors) of gun violence, or have parents serving jail sentences. In spite of these barriers, they have been, by typical measures, successful in their pursuit of a college education. Now, I sit at my own, very personal crossroads, with a brilliant son who has a developmental disability. This vulnerability is different than the kind I have seen in the students with whom I have worked, and at times, has left me feeling like I have little to offer.

FAITH IS THE SUBSTANCE OF THINGS HOPED FOR . . .

In spite of the strides and remaining challenges ahead—both in the landscape of American higher education and in our very personal lives—our faith still grounds our vision and expectations for our differently-abled son. This is what we do know. Avery does not have autism for Avery. He has autism, because we as parents, best friends, and Christians had our own personal limitations that demanded we do something differently—limitations in communicating, transparency, and lack of purpose. We are convinced Avery has autism because God has a purpose for this family and we needed to experience His will, love, and compassion for us in a way we had never experienced. Avery has autism because our testimony of hope and capacity for endurance needs to be developed and that any success we have needs to be directed to our faith in a real, tangible, and intimate relationship with Jesus Christ.

What we have to offer Avery is our prioritized love for God, our commitment to building families, our compassion for humanity, and our grounded faith that demands we keep pressing toward the mark for the prize of the high calling. What have we learned from this experience? We have learned that relationships work best when expectations are honestly and clearly communicated. We have learned that adaptability and flexibility are skills we absolutely need and are critical to our individual and collective success. We have been reminded that relationship reconciliation is exponentially more important than being right. And, that, at times, crying can be the best way to express our emotions.

Our family readily acknowledges that we benefit from social capital in ways that others do not. We are both second- and third-generation college graduates and our professional roles have helped us navigate this experience fairly effectively. But, we are reminded that no matter how much capital we possess, we cannot predict our life course. Regardless of the size of our network, our career success, or strength of our marriage, we know we will experience moments of intense doubt, frustration, and heartbreak because that is a part of the human experience. Thankfully, God knew who we were and who we were going to be as parents. He brought us together because we make a good team. And just like we can anticipate those moments of doubt, frustration, and heartbreak, we can also be confident that our faith allows us to equally anticipate and embrace the clarity, celebration, and love that are more salient than any challenge we might confront.

Our most recent pastor uses a poignant definition of faith that we cite quite often. He says faith is, "corresponding, suitable, appropriate action based on what God said out of His Word." As educators, the sentiment attached to this principle is very simple and applicable across contexts. We generally encourage parents to set high expectations for their children and create systems in which those expectations can be met through a delicate balance of challenge and support. As Christians, however, creating such a transformative experience requires us to match behavior, rhetoric, and testimony . . . and it's the only way we desire to make sense of this uniquely wonderful experience.

AUTHOR NOTE

Michael Hannon and LaChan Hannon are educators and co-founders of the Greater Expectations Teaching & Advocacy Center for Childhood Disabilities, Inc. (GETAC), which is a non-profit agency dedicated to supporting parents and children living with and caring for children with developmental disabilities.

You may contact GETAC at 133 Lincoln Avenue, State College, PA 16801. Tel.: (609) 694–8799. mhannon@getac.org

REFERENCES

American Psychiatric Association. (2000). *Diagnostic and statistical manual of mental disorders* (4th ed., Text Rev.). Washington, DC: American Psychiatric Association.

Blue Letter Bible, New Living Translation—1996–2012Retrieved February 27, 2012, from http://www.blueletterbible.org/Bible.cfm?b=Phl&c=1&t=NLT

Blue Letter Bible, New Living Translation—1996–2012 Retrieved February 27, 2012, from http://www.blueletterbible.org/Bible.cfm?b=Isa&c=53&t=KJV

Blue Letter Bible, New Living Translation—1996–2012 Retrieved February 27, 2012, from http://www.blueletterbible.org/Bible.cfm?b=Jam&c=2&t=KJV

Cook, L., Rumrill, P., & Tankersley, M. (2009). Priorities and understanding of faculty members regarding college students with disabilities. *International Society for Exploring Teaching and Learning, 21*(1), 84–96.

Grigal, M., & Hart, D. (Eds.). (2010). *Think college!: Postsecondary education options for students with intellectual disabilities.* Baltimore, MD: Brookes Publishing Company.

HEATH Resource Center. (1999). *1999 college freshmen with disabilities: A biennial statistical profile.* Washington, DC: Author.

Shaw, S. F., Madaus, J. W., & Dukes, L. L. (Eds.). (2010). *Preparing students with disabilities for college success: A practical guide to transition planning.* Baltimore, MD: Brookes Publishing Company.

Part II
Mothers

5 Extending a Hand
Grateful My Grandmother Raised Me

Cynthia (Ce) Garrison

The smell of collard greens, hockey pucks, "chikin' & dumplins," mashed potatoes, gravy, and warm scratch apple pie. The laughing chatter of familiarity. The wondrous feeling of a beaten path, summer hose playing, lemonade, horse riding, and rope swinging into Blue River. When I sit down to Sunday dinner, the rush comes back to me of the lazy summer days of bare feet and firefly catching.

My aunt, a strong and loud-mouthed woman, complains about some student whose parent has unsuccessfully tried to fight her grading. My cousin, new to the teaching ritual, considers both sides, but fails to speak against her mother. My grandma, proper and country, tells the way it used to be in a classroom, and the way her mother used to do things. The men are sitting, comfortably tuned out, and focused on a delicious feast. It was as if my times on the outskirts of Savannah, Georgia, were preparing me for what lie ahead. I began to respect the closeness of family and what Sunday dinner really meant. To me, family dinner is symbolic of culture. It is the place where we all gather to get to know each other all over again. Every Sunday, we sit down different than we were the week before. To me, culture is a process of learning who you are by understanding those who helped make you.

My family still says grace like great grandma did. We are not as religious as she was; in fact, I do not claim Christianity, but Buddhism, but I say the prayer in her memory, and I say it slowly to take in all the passion it embodies.

> Our Father who art in heaven, hallowed be thy name. Thy kingdom come. Thy will be done on earth as it is in heaven. Give us this day our daily bread, and forgive us our trespasses, as we forgive those who trespass against us, and lead us not into temptation, but deliver us from evil. For thine is the kingdom, and the power, and the glory, for ever and ever. Amen.

Somehow, when those final words leave my mouth, a part of me feels solid. Somewhere between my heart and my growling stomach, I feel a connection. Loud Sinatra classics blaring in my head, the taste of stamp adhesive, a good '80s hairdo flashes before my eyes. It is all inside of me. From it spawned a mouthy 19-year-old with an untamed spirit, and a respect for what once had to happen for me to be here.

In 1912, 1944, 1962, and 1982 four generations of women began. My great-grandmother spoke of the Crash and World War II, my grandmother of Vietnam and Woodstock, my aunt of the '80s and perestroika in the Cold War. My cousin and I live to tell of the Middle Eastern conflict and the new millennium. My great-grandmother called her time the "glory days." Growing up in Chicago, she remembers when her parents would dance to Sinatra or the excitement when they bought a dishwasher for the first time. Soon after, money was worthless and the man she would marry was peddling newspapers on the street to make money for an engagement ring. When World War II broke out, my great-grandfather, an ordained Methodist minister, moved his family to southern Indiana, where his brother's family lived. Called by the draft, he left two boys at home and one on the way. My grandfather was the oldest boy. He remembers his mother going to the family church every day and praying for the safe return of her husband. I remember my great-grandmother telling me that the power of faith outweighs the power of guns and of hatred and of all the things in the world that keep us from love.

My great-grandmother made my heritage important for me. She inspired me through her everlasting love and passion for family and for friends. My grandfather reminds me of his mother's commitment to family every time he calls the family to dinner, and they talk about the things my great-grandma loved about her family. Probably inspired by his mother, my grandfather had a love for strong women. Perhaps that's why he married my grandmother. Her life was a constant struggle. Raising two kids in Savannah, Georgia, in the '60s and '70s was no easy feat. My grandparents raised their family in the poorest neighborhood in Savannah, running a 7-Eleven on the block, and no family nearby. My grandpa was an insurance salesman by day, and a store clerk at night. My grandma was a store clerk by day, and a mother at night. She took as much care as she could. Her children always had clean clothes and a home-cooked meal, just like her mother had always taught her.

When my father died just 3 short years after I was born, my grandmother took it hardest. It was like a part of her went missing. Her whole life had been given up to take care of this man and now, beyond her control, his life had been taken from him. My biological mother gave me away shortly after my father died. She has had no influence on my development. She kept my brothers and sisters, and I was the one child she gave up. The truth? I had a mom. My grandmother was my mom. I am her child in everything that I do. I even visit Walmart in the same way she does. I vow and declare to go in for one thing, but I come out with 10 more. I have her diligence and her reason, I gained her maternal instinct. When I talk, people will tell me, "That's exactly what Bev would say."

My grandmother fought her way through high school in a one room schoolhouse, having to quit college several times when money was scarce, children needed raising, or the call for help came from others. In December of 2005, my grandma finally received her Ph.D. in special education. She told me,

> For my generation, women had to be twice as smart and work twice as hard as a man to be recognized for their ability. You have watched me study all your life. You watched me receive my doctorate at an age when most people would say it was a waste of time. Follow your dream, even if it takes longer than you had planned. Life happens. Don't use trials as an excuse to not do.

I think this statement is culture to me. Culture is something handed down from one generation—a memory to sustain the legacy of where someone came from and whom they once were. I remember watching my grandma study. I remember countless Saturdays of licking stamps and sticking them on envelopes to send to people she needed to survey. I remember being the last kid in school almost every night waiting for her to finish being the teacher, so when she went home, she could be the student.

HOME IS WHERE THE HEART IS

When I was a teenager we moved back to our family's land of origin—Indiana. I used to be very sad when we moved back to Indiana from Georgia. I understood why we did it. My great-grandparents were getting older, and my great-aunt needed to be looked after. To me, Indiana was a dirt path leading to nowhere. Everything was so "country." People talked in a non-Southern country voice. They spit, spun their tires, hung out at the farmer's market, and flew rebel flags (a tradition that is still lost on me). I could not stand to be associated with them.

Now, I consider it a part of me. With time, the Georgia accent faded, I learned how to spit, and I raised a "mean" prize-winning cow. I loved everything about my farmland—the way it smelled, the way the people knew each other, the community that was built on the understanding that everything belonged to everybody. I began to see that there was a difference between country folk and "redneck hicks." I learned how to rope swing into a "crick." I hope that one day I will raise children to the same standards. I hope they will be respectful, but inquisitive. I wish them all the Sinatra blaring, stamp taste, hair towers, and plain old country common sense that they can stomach. I hope that I can inspire other people to find their family, even if a mother and a father are not in the dynamic. I want them to remember that life happens, but that they should never let that stand in the way of what really matters.

Finally, I hope that one day my own children will know the amount of love from which they have been built. I hope they know what it means to not only live in the moment, but also to remember the past. I hope I can be as wonderful in their eyes as my grandmother is in mine, and her mother was in hers. I hope I can live up to the legacy and keep it going. "For thine is the kingdom, and the power, and the glory for ever and ever. Amen."

6   Mama Says
Activist, Pedagogue, and Feminist?

Crystal Leigh Endsley with Clara Endsley

INTRODUCTION

My mother, who has made her living for the last 8 years minding other people's children, gives me instructions on how to raise the children I don't have yet. . . . *Make sure you live close by me when you get pregnant. It will make things easier for both of us.*

My mother, who never set foot in a college, has dispensed more practical wisdom for living than any textbook I've read. . . . *Never let them see you sweat. You just smile through it all. And let God take care of the rest. He knows how to get folks back better than you.*

My mother, who used to fuss at me for not eating enough, now tells me to stay skinny as long as I can. . . . *Don't listen to them when they tease you. You are perfect. You can't please everyone so the only person you need to be concerned about pleasing is the Lord . . . and your Mama.*

My mother, who has never seen me on stage is the greatest performer I know. . . . *Don't leave the house looking like a ragamuffin or without your lipstick. The day you do will be the day you run into everybody you know and then they will have something to talk about! You may not have a dollar in your pocket but you don't have to dress or act like it!*

My mother. I still can't figure out if we're on two roads to the same place or on the same road going in two different directions.

MAMA, CAN WE TALK?

I have had many conversations with a rich variety of women from my campus who have all expressed an aching homesickness, a feeling of displacement and a lack of belonging in the classroom and campus community. Overwhelmingly, these women all feel an intense and unrelenting craving for the comfort of their mothers. These emotions have led to discussions about the difference between the educational space that we now occupy and the home place from which we came; the lives that we now lead and those that our Mamas experienced. How in the world did we end up *here*, we wonder, and why isn't there anything new our mothers can tell us to ease the aggravation we feel? How can they help us manage the audacity to want everything— family and degrees, understanding and independence? Tears and laughter, sometimes all at once, usually accompany these conversations and we try to encourage one another. We tell each other that although there isn't a handbook or guideline to follow, we received enough thorough "home training" from our mothers that has equipped us to do our jobs. We appreciate and miss our mothers. Most of all, we ache to hear their voices.

Well, I'm flattered I'm sure, but my story isn't that exciting.

In her article entitled "Writing Ethnographic Narratives," Linda Brodkey (1987) writes,

> One studies stories not because they are true or even because they are false, but for the same reason that people tell and listen to them, in order to learn about the terms on which others make sense of their lives: what they take into account and what they do not; what they consider worth contemplating and what they do not; what they are and are not willing to raise and discuss as problematic and unresolved in life. (p. 47)

When I first asked MamaMama to allow me to interview her and use her responses in my work, I was most interested in learning about the choices that she made as a mother and how those choices continue to shape the educated woman that I am becoming. It is not the true or false that I seek, rather it is the "why" in MamaMama's life that I want answered.

I have never before asked permission to quote my mother directly or to examine her words publicly and she was both flattered and full of nervous questions about the process. She wanted full editorial rights, a list of who would be reading it, and most of all to make sure that I wasn't just trying "to put her business in the street." I had to think long and hard about what topics were worth approaching. My mother and I talk often and for lengthy periods of time so engaging a conversation wouldn't be difficult. But, as with any relationship, the topics that matter are often sensitive and personal. This requires that I consider such issues as loyalty and respect for my MamaMama's privacy and reputation. I don't want to embarrass Mama-Mama or myself and I am a little bit afraid that this process is going to hurt. What if I learn things I don't want to know? What if I get no answers and no indication that I'm on the right track? What if I'm wrong and the fear that I have no right to be here turns out to be a reality?

To be honest, I never thought much about how MamaMama learned about herself before now. But, at some point, I realized that it was important to understand how she learned if I really wanted to understand how I learned from her. The ways we learn often determine the ways we teach others. If I can analyze the content and understand the approach that she has used to teach me, then I will hopefully begin to understand why I care so much about teaching what I teach and why I teach the way that I do. In accepting that I am a teacher and a "producer of knowledge" I am also recognizing Mama-Mama as such. MamaMama has always been my teacher, you see. Clara Jean Flowers Endsley, a 44-year-old white housewife, does not share identical experiences with me, Crystal Leigh Endsley, her 25-year-old mixed-race, college-educated daughter. But she has still equipped me to live sanely and successfully in this world of academia—a place that is foreign to her. Understanding and respecting MamaMama's position as a knowledge producer opens up the possibility that, in this role, MamaMama trained me to produce similar knowledge and to recognize certain kinds of experience-based knowledge as worth having. Although I'm not looking for "right or wrong" answers, I want to know how I got my ideas about what counts as "right" and "wrong." If I can learn the ways MamaMama makes sense of her life, how she makes her choices, and what she finds important, then perhaps I can learn how she gave those skills to me. More importantly, I can better see how her life experience informs my own leadership practices in the classroom and other areas of my life. I wanted to make better sense of MamaMama, in order to make better sense of myself.

In her book entitled *Feminism Is For Everybody*, bell hooks (2000) opens the text by explaining the motivation that propelled her to write that particular book at that particular time: "I had to write it because I kept waiting for it to appear, and it did not" (p. ix). hooks describes the longing she felt for many years to tell the real and unapologetic story of women. It is with a similar longing that I have been compelled to write on the topic of mothers and daughters. I am writing this chapter because this story, the story of my MamaMama and myself, will not appear unless I write it. I do not want to wait any longer. I wanted to get to the root of what Luttrell (1997) defines as "common sense" which "recognizes and validates the knowledge that grows out of life experience" (p. 26). If I can understand *what* Mama has tried to teach me with great effort (common sense) and *how* she taught me (home training) then perhaps I will be able to figure out *why* I do the things that I do as a woman, scholar, and artist. I am interested in the idea of legacy—I didn't pop out of the womb ready to fight for social justice and waving a feminist banner. How did I learn to respond in difficult situations? How much does the rest of my life have to do with the beginnings of it?

MAMA KNOWS BEST

At the time that I started this project, I was in pursuit of a doctoral degree: first generation, first woman, and first woman of color in my family to take these steps. When I arrived at grad school it was as if I couldn't type a single paper without Mama finding her way into the text. How did this woman, whose experiences were so different from mine, whose position in life was so different from mine, permeate every conversation I had? I found myself quoting her constantly: "Well, Mama says . . . My Mama says . . . you know what Mama says" using her voice as the voice of authority. Sometimes I even put my own words in Mama's mouth. Infusing my words with her tone lends them a heavier weight. The ears of my friends, students, and teachers perk up when they know that my mother said such and such. By invoking Mama to speak for me instead of stating my own opinion, I call upon the intense relationships that other people share with their own mothers. Respect, longing, reverence, adoration, and fear all surface with thoughts of mothers. People pause and think twice about disputing their Mama. After all, if Mama said it that means it must be true, right? Mamas don't lie, do they?

See, even the Lord has a sense of humor: The truth comes out in jokes.

Yes, the need for a sense of humor was never as evident as it is now when stress, loneliness, and financial strain threaten to press bits of joy out of my life. So I look at pictures of my family and I read the hilarious e-mails containing the latest potty-training success stories of my nephews. I can't be with my Mama right now, so I write papers about her. I can't articulate the way I feel for my family, so instead I perform monologues about them. I cannot be around the people who have loved me the longest, so I work to be indispensable to my job and try to extend myself to friends and students at school so that they will love me or at least like me real hard. The collage of writing contained in this chapter is a collection of e-mails, phone conversations, and memories that Mama and I have shared. Our relationship is by no means perfect, but I have seen her under many different types of pressures and circumstances and when I have felt the urge to explode, she has remained gracious. I figured that it made more sense to use Mama as my main source because she raised me based on her beliefs. My sensibilities come from the training I received from her. You are my full moon, Mama, and you shine much brighter than I ever could.

Don't worry about being a star. Be like the moon and let the world see only your bright side.

THE CONVERSATIONS

Mama on Activism

My idea of being an activist is being involved. Making a difference in someone's life. Caring about the end result and how people are treated and viewed. I have two precious grandsons that I just adore. Malik is 3 and Ramiro is almost 2. I want them to have the many opportunities

*that are afforded in our community. Because of finances, they can-
not join expensive children's play gyms or go to private schools. They
cannot even afford pre-school, which is not required in our state. I
find other resources for them to grow and learn in our area. The local
library is a great place for children to learn to interact and develop
skills learned in pre-school. The park is also good for exercise and
social skill development. The museums in our area provide stimula-
tion and are enjoyable for everyone in the family. Sand and water play
can be done at the beach with dollar store toys. It just takes a little
footwork to find what is available for children. I'm glad I'm the one
who gets to take care of them while their mother and father work. My
two little grandsons are mixed. They are beautiful boys and I want
them to know they are somebody special. I teach them to succeed in
every area—even potty training! They will have equal opportunities
because we search out what is available and take advantage of the
resources our community offers to those in their age group. They will
have the loving foundation to try new things and when they mess up,
to try again and again and again.*

These are Mama's own words describing herself as active in a very material way. Mama takes pride in claiming responsibility for another generation
of our family. She speaks of what the grandchildren will have because of
"our" search to find opportunities available to them. Mama implies here
that the whole family, no matter their position, is responsible for these efforts
to create a beloved community realizing dreams of freedom and justice, living the truth that we are all created equal (hooks, 2003, p. x). Mama is
proud to be a leader in the formation of this loving foundation of which she
speaks. Although Mama isn't licensed to teach and her grandchildren are
not enrolled in an official pre-school, she is committed to her unofficial role
as a teacher in their lives. Mama's self-identified commitment as caretaker
and teacher of her grandsons posits the knowledge that she contributes as a
priority and she calls upon her skills to protect and educate the boys in every
area. Wendy Luttrell (1997) identifies this knowledge as common sense: "all-
encompassing . . . abilities to make ends meet; solve family, work, or community disputes; overcome natural disasters; and avoid racial conflict" (p.
32). Mama's ability and efforts at multi-tasking so that everyone's needs are
met are both a burden and a source of pride where she demonstrates skills for
coping, surviving, and providing for her family.

I was married when I was 18 years old. I had two small babies by the
time I was 19. I married a man much older than I. He joined the Navy
soon after we were married. During deployments, I was required to
continue on with life and daily activities. I made decisions that affected
the entire family. I leaned heavily upon God. I knew that with His love
and acceptance, I could do anything. I gained much needed confidence

and learned that I had the ability to carry on and make quality decisions. My husband allowed me to take responsibility for the family. I chose the place of worship we attended. I handled the finances without having to ask permission or questions. No one was looking over my shoulder to frown or approve my decisions. As our children entered school, I learned to talk to people and to face challenges. I beefed up my negotiation skills at yard sales and flea markets. It gave me such freedom to choose for myself and form my own opinions.

In fact, Mama wasn't choosing only for herself, she was choosing for our whole family. There's nothing like being forced into a situation to speed the development of your skills. Although she did not technically earn the finances, she was still responsible for them. This is another example of the particular type of knowledge common sense refers to: one that is validated because it is grown out of life experience (Luttrell, 1997). Mama did not take classes beyond high school, instead she developed life skills based partially on what she had learned and partially on the information and opinions she formed through personal experience. Although the application of her common sense knowledge was certainly a chore she viewed as duty and obligation, it was also the space where she discovered autonomy for herself. She also remarks on not having to ask "permission" when it came to money, but in the same breath describes how her husband "allowed" her to take responsibility for the family. The truth of the matter is that Daddy was in no position to do anything else. Their marriage *had* to be a partnership of trust because he was on a boat thousands of miles away. Her desire and push for me to be self-sufficient is a clear indication that she believes financial independence equals mobility and power and that mobility and power are goals worth working toward.

Valerie Walkerdine (1986) speaks in a helpful way to the contradictions wrapped up within the position of motherhood by suggesting that one of the main duties of motherhood includes guarding a moral code through which children are to be taught and raised. Although there is undoubtedly power steeped in the position of mother, this power also puts the woman in an incredibly vulnerable position to be judged and evaluated. Mama is glad that she is the one who gets to be the caretaker for Malik and Ramiro because this means she gets to make decisions and assume an active role in their upbringing. But Walkerdine reminds us that the role of the powerful always comes with a price, for being a guardian is a responsibility that is inescapable and like all public positions of power, it is also judged harshly. Although I certainly agree that an unbelievable and unrealistic amount of pressure is put on women to demonstrate an innate sensibility as a caretaker, I can still appreciate the opportunity that resides in a mothering space. What better place exists to develop strategies to invoke practical and material changes in the social structures that force these women into such positions in the first place? It's ironic that Mama acknowledges and enjoys being powerful in the space between motherhood and grandmotherhood. Socially, these roles were not designed to position her as powerful. The circumstances of motherhood that were meant to freeze her movement and growth, when inverted, have formed the network of support and resource-fulness that she used to propel not only herself, but her daughter into new territory. Mama's power is one that she uses to serve. There is an element of sacrifice that blinks steadily from the midst of Mama's actions that both saddens and inspires me. I wonder if it is enough for her to see me move in ways she did not—is she satisfied with her life? Am I satisfied with mine? Just as Mama cannot trade places with me, neither can I shift gears in mid-stride. Will we be content living vicariously through one another's tales of life in a parallel world? And if so, why do I always feel like I'm missing out on something that is on the other side?

> *I am always amazed when you perform and speak in front of others. I see a part of you that is not projected every day. I see the passion you have for what you believe in. I hear the compassion for people in your words. I see your performances as you using your God-given talent to reach others. Yes, that is an activist; it just may not be everyone's definition of feminist or activist.*

Mama lists several characteristics here in her definition of what it means to be an activist. According to Mama, "passion," "compassion," and "reaching others" are three traits that should manifest themselves in activism. Michelle Fine (1992) defines a feminist activist as someone who will "press, provoke, and unbalance social inequities that choreograph relations of gender, race, class, disability, and sexuality" (p. i). Fine also states that feminist politics, research, and activism "grow out of the lived politics of women before me" as well as "women who lived the lives they were supposed to live . . . and paid dearly" (p. xi). It is the "lived politics" that Fine refers to here that matches Mama's example. Mama has only her own experience as any proof that her "pressing and provoking" has challenged injustice. She freely discusses issues of socioeconomics and class—that finances might limit the educational resources and experiences available to the boys. However, she only mentions in passing that her grandsons are mixed race and how that compels her to let them know they are "somebody special." Her singular reference to race indicates that she understands the potentially negative social implications that being mixed can have for her grandsons. However, Mama's unwilling-ness to elaborate on the multitude of issues derived from race and racism that are embedded in her statement reflect a desire for the boys to succeed despite social restrictions and a refusal to discuss a subject with which she is either uncomfortable or thinks is unnecessary.

I found it surprising that Mama attributed her confidence to her role in her marriage because marriage is so often described as a sacrifice of a woman's independence and a deferment of her dreams and plans. I half expected her to admit she resented having my brother and me so young and getting married at all. She has told me the story of the job she had as a senior in high school as a buyer in a trendy boutique. Her employers had arranged to pay for her college tuition if she continued her work there. When she discovered she was pregnant, they fired her. I continued to question Mama about her ideas on marriage because I thought she would tell me not to get married, but to stay single and free as long as possible. But, this did not happen. Instead, it was in her husband's house that she was thrust into a role of independence and decision making—a powerful role she never played in her father's house. I find it interesting that it was only within the very structure of the family that Fine suggests would limit her power that Mama actually found the opportunity and occasion to grow as an activist. I also want to point out that although Mama has no problem with asserting herself on behalf of her family, she does not feel entitled by herself. Mama's self-worth is not separate from her children or her grandchildren. It saddens me that she cannot see that standing on her own she is valuable. Before writing this paper, I didn't understand that I was her status symbol simply because she didn't think she was good enough on her own. I think of the times when I have taken for granted the ways in which she has sacrificed for me. I think of the incidents when she has gone without having her very basic needs met so that I could have something extra. Like the time that she sent me a completely unnecessary pair of red shoes for my birthday just because she knew that the obnoxious frivolity of wearing 4-inch heels in the snow would make me laugh. She fusses at me for giving too much to people, money that I don't have or material things that I need, but she forgets that giving is how she shows she loves me.

Although Mama's life has taken a traditional path, it would be a mistake to describe her as submissive, a doormat, or a meek acceptor of prescribed white femininity because through her actions and choices she deliberately tested such roles (Dehli, 1991). In her writings about the struggle between maternal relations and the academy, Lubna Nazir Chaudhry (2000) succinctly states, "the terms of resistance and bids for empowerment emerge out of the specific circumstances of a particular life and who is to say what terms and which bids are more efficacious" (p. 106)? Who has the right to assess a mother's agency? That is the beauty of discovering Mama as an activist and the power in articulating her experiences in a different setting—perhaps there is a way to use her methods or modes of thinking in a similar way while in my location as a scholar.

Mama's work is not in the eye of the public, it is not loud or likely to get noticed. She does not dress or speak in a way that would trigger thoughts of revolution. Her power is in the "ordinary," in the daily dependability she provides. For there is a different kind of activism that takes place on a personal level that Mama clearly exerts for the sake of her family. Patricia Hill Collins (1991) offers a definition of activism that compels us to "rethink" how the term is typically used. On a fundamental level, Collins defines

activism as a way of living everyday life that makes it possible for one
to survive using self-definition, self-valuation, and movement toward self-
reliance. Defining one's self and making decisions that prioritize the values
evident in my home training is at the core of this lived activism. Speaking
to the absence of black women in formal authoritarian roles and their lack
of membership at the forefront of political organizations, Collins offers
us a view of activism that takes place in everyday life; an activism that is
accessible to all of us no matter our station in life (Collins, 1991). This daily
practice of resistance is often more difficult to maintain because the effects
are deceptively small. There is no parade, no campaign, no applause for the
traditional stay-at-home mother who struggles to feed and clothe her kids
properly—to ensure that they don't have to live the way she has. To be an
activist on Mama's terms is exhausting. There is something to be said for
the strength in women who survive their lives, for those who do not just
learn the skill set of doing certain things, but also learn to enjoy, and find
beauty and purpose while doing them (McWilliam, 2000). To honor the
discipline within this sort of strength is also to honor the dignity of the
women in the completion of tasks that no one else wanted or was willing
to do. This activism is a quiet one; it begins as a private activity where not
even the brief reward of fame is reckoned. Mama's activism and the theory
within it is something I would like to refer to as "home training."

> *When I was growing up, I was never encouraged to continue my edu-
> cation. I was never told I could do anything. Oh my parents loved
> me. I knew that. But . . . I had an older brother and I was continually
> told that I couldn't do this or that because I was a girl. I couldn't go
> camping. I couldn't ride the mini bike trail. I couldn't play football. I
> did not grow up being confident in myself and my abilities. I acquired
> that after I was married. When we encouraged you to go to college, we
> were interested at first in you being able to get a good job in case you
> ever had to support yourself and children. This world is not stable and
> you cannot depend on this world and the systems in it. I thought that
> by you getting a good education, you would always have a job skill to
> fall back on when you married and found yourself in need. You have
> grown to be more than I ever dreamed. And I know there is more to
> come. I just hope that when you have children, you will live close by so
> I can enjoy them as much as I have enjoyed your brother's two boys.*

Mama's distrust of the institutions and "systems" of this world are interesting to me. Although Mama's current position (and by position I mean
white, newly middle class, housewife) may not appear to be transgressive
enough to warrant the title of "feminist," her wariness of the institutions
in society (including higher education) indicate a suspicion that they are
dangerous. Although she recognizes the benefit of these institutions for the
social mobility they can potentially provide, and therefore encourages me

in my pursuit of a degree, it is only her desire for me to protect myself that drives her support. I don't want Mama to feel that she has to defend herself from me or from what I have learned from other teachers. I wonder why I should believe what she says when she encourages me to go as far as I can in my academic career when she repeatedly expresses her own suspicions of what I'm learning and how I'm beginning to translate the world. Mama exhibits both a certain sense of awe and intimidation when I begin sharing what I'm learning with her. The power shift in our own relationship feels so *wrong* and *backwards* to me. I find myself hiding and repressing and denying my desire to teach her what I know now because of my own awkward uncertainty with the transposing of roles in our relationship.

I get scared when I have to really make an effort to *relate* to my family. The lives we lead are so different and the choices that I make are a result of boundaries that encase me, boundaries that Mama could never understand because she has not had the same experience. When I visit home excited about my new theories, my campus programs, and my new academic life, Mama never ceases to question the very root of what I am doing. Over the summer I was home and the day before I left, Mama said to me, "Crystal, me and your Daddy were talking and we were just wondering where you are." Confused, I asked what she meant. "I mean, I've seen little glimpses of you since you've been home, but I was just wondering where Crystal was at? I'm glad you made friends at school, but don't forget to be who you are." Immediately I grew defensive and tears came to my eyes. What does it mean when even Mama does not recognize me? She asked me if being an actor meant that I was always on stage. I was hurt that she thought I was pretending and I was scared that she was right. Her question was genuine and not meant to wound me. I began to question who I had allowed myself to become. I have worried that Mama is stuck, that she has no agency or mobility and the very thought of a life like hers both seduces and suffocates me. We don't stand in agreement with one another's choices or politics. And just as I often imagine the possibilities of a lifestyle for her that would somehow seem more bearable to me, I discovered that Mama uses her imagination for me, too. This is why it's so important to me to expand the notion of activism and feminism so that she is included. In her essay "Excuse Me While I Explode," E. S. Maduro (2002) addresses these same feelings of contradiction:

> I feel angry at the confusion of adoring my mother, of thinking she is a phenomenal woman who raised her children with grace and style, of thinking I would give anything to be like her . . . and at the same time, looking down on her for all the things she quietly accepted, and knowing that I want to be nothing like that. (p. 9)

Maduro speaks to the intersection of admiration and irritation that exists when there is both a desire to be *like* someone and at the same time to be *bigger* than someone, meaning to surpass the station in life they inhabit, to find a way to live my dreams and still honor hers. I want to spread out more. I want to carry the best of the academy back home to Mama and also transport whomever from my family is interested in traveling with me through school. I am beginning to understand that where we live does not have to determine or limit the actions we take. It was Mama's imagination, her concepts of what she wanted and didn't necessarily have that led her to raise me to occupy a space that was located beyond her boundaries—even beyond her belief. While I am here in central Pennsylvania, it is my Mama's e-mails and phone calls and super-long voicemails that keep my feet (and focus) firmly planted in the red clay of Louisiana's dirt roads. Don't let Mama's outside appearance fool you; after all it was she who first taught me to be an actor. It is she who is the subversive one, who taught me to work both within and against (St. Pierre, 2000).

Mama on Living Arrangements

In my search for a new place to belong what I found instead was where I could *not* belong. Anne-Louise Brookes's (1992) work around family, self, abuse, and storytelling speaks of a similar awakening. At one point in her academic career, Brookes realized that educational institutions do not teach us to discuss or even conceptualize what might be considered socially unacceptable or theoretically insignificant. What am I to do when the "socially unacceptable and insignificant" include my home and family? You see, I have come to understand that as Dehli (1991) explains, the experiences and histories of people of color and the working class are often intentionally ignored because their validity could prove to be a threat to the existing structures that give the "Ivory Tower" its power (p. 51). People like me are not supposed to be here and that's the bottom line. I wondered what it might mean to me, both personally and professionally, to write about these things in the very context of the academy that demands that I choose a place to call home. This choice comes either at the cost of a degree that will equip me to take the next step into my life or to live as an outsider to my family by further separating from them. I could not understand why, up until this point, I was made to feel that the talks with my mother were improper or inadequate bases for academic knowledge (Dehli, 1991). I could not understand the logic behind the methods with which I was being trained throughout my schooling experiences because it was those conversations with Mama that directly informed how I process, analyze, and produce my own scholarship. It was her training that was determining what I research and my methods for teaching. Mama is the reason I pursued higher education. Now, the very thing I have to contribute to the academy, my reverence for my family, the academy demands that I forfeit.

It was at this point that I realized that I was not only feeling pressure from the academy to choose where I would call home, where my loyalties in the form of energy, time, and focus would reside, but a similar pressure was coming from home. Despite her urgings for me to "be the best" and to "reach for the sky," Mama has very clear expectations that those aspirations will be achieved based on certain spiritual and ethical conditions and an expectation to serve the needs of my family, both present and future. Mama has told me before how tired she gets of hearing about everything she's doing wrong when I come home; she has teasingly said she pities my students and my coworkers because of my tendency to impassioned outbursts.

> *Girl, don't forget you aren't just representing yourself up there, you stand for all of us. Now, you have to make up your mind as to who you are working for. You can't serve two masters.*

I am finally relieved to understand as Rockhill (as cited in Brookes, 1992) suggests, "that what I've experienced for so long as a personal split, and a severe sense of personal inadequacy, is anything but personal. It is produced by the very structure of academe in which we are bound" (p. 322). Although I would argue that the division Rockhill speaks of is both a structure and deeply personal, I now understand that I am not the sole cause or product of this gap. After all my fuss and efforts to be accepted either at home or at school, what often happens immediately upon that acceptance is that I feel pressure to choose between the two. I realize that I am one of a great number of students who feel the pull of home—this understanding only deepens my sense of responsibility to make the issues of one side relevant to the other. I have become my home. Mama's interest in activism and an exploration, albeit tentative, of feminism was initiated because of the books she has read from readings lists I've sent her from school, or from the papers of mine she has read or performances or lectures I have shared with her. Slowly, she has discovered that she "enjoys relating academic material to herself" (Brookes, 1992, p. 50). She remains unconvinced of her feminist qualities, but her words and her efforts to instruct me based on her own production of a specific knowledge that consciously resists an oppressive, racist male-centered power structure are proof that she is, in spite of her disbelief, a feminist pedagogue.

Mama on Living a Life of Purpose

> *The emptiest barrel makes the most noise—people talk the most about what they are lacking or what they want most. After a while, talking don't do any good—either do something or be quiet.*

There are lessons to be learned from this woman who has not had access or extended interest in the academy, who thus far has benefitted little from the majority of work that gets developed here. Mama is the reason I try to match my academic and artistic work to the belief that "philosophy must matter to the non-philosopher"—in other words, academic, artistic, and political work must contribute to the betterment of the home community (St. Pierre, 2000). My work must matter to the communities that have allowed me to reach for the sky. And as Mama says, I must use their strength to anchor me. My goals are not better than Mama's, but they are different despite her influence. No matter where we come from or where we are going, life ain't no easy ride, nor is it a ride we take on our own.

In the surprising discovery of exactly how strong of an attachment to my home community, namely my Mama, that I have, I uncovered this voice of mine. In this fight to make the social issues, these deeply personal and very concrete realities that face my nephews and my brother and my parents, matter, I think of my students. To rouse the attention of those students that are pre-service teachers and who exhibit a blatant lack of concern for the poor in our communities, I call up my memory of home. I use my position to speak up and remember the working class from which I have been removed. In my separation from my Mama and my community, I have come to signify that very community in the new places where I work, learn, and perform—whether I mean to or not.

   Build a bridge honey, and get over it!

There is a Bible verse Mama quotes often: "so is my word that goes out from my mouth: It will not return to me empty, but will accomplish what I desire and achieve the purpose for which I sent it" (Isaiah 55:11, New International Bible, 1984). Bronwyn Davies (2000) agrees that we speak and write the unknown into existence. She continues "we need to write and speak utopias, we need to rewrite the past and the present, we need to write and speak all of ourselves" (p. 54). Juxtaposing feminist theorist Davies with an Old Testament prophet might seem a far reach, but the ideas in both of these quotes are the same: There is power in the spoken and written word. Through the act of speaking and writing about current circumstances and about the living conditions we desire we are able to deconstruct and rebuild the past and present in meaningful ways.

This is why writing with and about Mama helps me learn about myself. I have learned and changed since writing and performing and claiming language as my own. Here I have begun to unlearn the parts of myself that I initially learned as undesirable or negative because they cause me to be different and therefore difficult. My perspectives as a performer, a chameleon of characters, an unconventional teacher, a "care giver," a working class woman of color, an inhabitant of ambiguity, a fighter, a boundary breaker, have been rearranged in a positive light. I have learned to reconstitute language, "to reclaim and re-write untold histories, to subvert what counts as knowledge and truth, and to challenge those who claim authority" (St.

Pierre, 2000, p. 5). I thought if Mama felt that her words were welcomed and valuable, if she would trust me with them, then maybe she could get a boost, too. Maybe she could rediscover the love of English she told me she felt in high school. I wanted to offer her the chance to describe herself just the way she wanted without fearing anyone's opinion or preconceived ideas about who she is or should be. Speaking and believing positively about ourselves in spite of fear are important feminist acts because when we define ourselves there is less room for a negative definition to get circulated and believed. I wanted to share this validating part of my academic experience with her. She deserves it.

Because Mama did finally agree to this collaborative work, she also agreed to share the spotlight with me. Mama has taken the stage in a reproduction of her own knowledge and experiences. I have explained that her agreement to be at the center of this research paper implicates her as a feminist knowledge producer, as a person who believes all people are created equally, is aware of her knowledge production, and who does so with the deliberate intention of exposing and deconstructing misogynistic and destructive myths about women. She did not think it did.

> *(laughing) Crystal, you're being dramatic. I didn't say anything about being a feminist. I don't know about all that. All I said was that I would answer your questions as honestly as I can.*

It is important to look at why Mama feels the category of feminist does not include her. Her tone of voice made it very clear to me that she did not feel safe. I briefly wondered if I had scared her with the accounts I recited about my own trials in graduate school. I wanted this paper to be a secure place where Mama and ideally others are able to hear echoes of their own voices. There is personal validation that comes from seeing your words printed in text. This paper could be a connection between my two worlds of family and the academy—the ultimate parent–teacher conference. Even if she was uncomfortable with some of the subject matter, Mama did think that it was important to examine her experiences and to tell her side of her own story. She also agreed when I said that I can't get to where I'm going if I don't know where I've been—or where *she* had been before me. Plus, she enjoys the idea of "a woman like her" sneaking into academia, a place hitherto forbidden.

I explained to Mama that there was a chance that no one other than she, my advisor, and I would read this—that her storytelling might not ever get included in mainstream bodies of knowledge such as magazines, journals, or Lifetime movies. She laughed when I said that our experience might not be sexy enough to sell to popular culture. It is still important to do work around the lackluster and very daily parts of our lives because it is in these spaces that we discover the effects of what *is* included in the mainstream. I explained that we could create the opportunity to assert ourselves as valid and valuable, although maybe never popular.

BECOMING MAMA

As I stated earlier, I asked Mama to join me in this paper in order to offer her a different possibility of viewing herself. Because she is my mother, I do not view Mama or her life choices as insignificant. However, I know well the humiliation of not being taken seriously by an outside world. Through jointly writing this piece, we are creating the chance that others (and/or we) might recognize their voices, hear parts of their own lives, or find hope in some of our ideas. After all, people have been seeking out Mama's voice for years. I think about my high school and middle school friends and how they came to my house even when I wasn't there just to sit and talk to my Mama and Daddy. The sanctuary they were looking for was available to them at no charge in the Navy housing projects where we lived. There was no offering plate being passed around, no donation needed, no tuition to be paid—just come as you are and get a little comfort. I was lucky enough to have Mama, with her expansive heart, her sensitivity to hurting people and her gift of teaching and advising. And so as I try to figure out the best possible way to guide the young women that now seek me out as a mentor and teacher, I am called to remember the phrases my Mama would say to me. At home I find myself doing little things around the kitchen like Mama does, or laughing and thinking I sound like her echo. I know in that moment that I am taking up the mantle Mama has so carefully stitched together for me. And in those moments, I feel lonesome. I miss both who me and Mama were and the vision of what I hope we will become. There are moments that I wish she could be here with me, experiencing what I am so that her life could be fuller. I wish that she could have a moment to glimpse whom she could have been had she chosen to go to school or not get married or lead a different life. There are moments when I think that all of her talents, street smarts, and sharp practicality have been wasted on a life as a sometime-housewife or in the role of the supporter in the family. I appreciate her bravery sharing her story with me—the process of becoming Mama. And the deliberate choices she made in spite of the odds and the raw pain have been the very reason that I can become more. It was my Mama who taught me that even the smallest of actions do speak the loudest. She taught me the art of the thank you note and the power of a home baked good. She taught me how to cherish the elderly because we need them just as badly as they need us. Mama leads by example. As I reflect on the experience of becoming a student all over again, appreciating and writing with and about Mama, I am reminded of Elizabeth St. Pierre's (2000) reflections about her research in a small faith-infused community of women who made no effort to change their status in life, "Who am I to judge those who pray over me so sweetly? Who am I to desire a different life for them?" (p. 270). Who am I indeed?

> *When you are hurting or lost, the safest place to be is home. To love someone, to love yourself, is to learn to forgive. Forgiveness and being*

quick to turn to God are what will get you through the hardest times of your life. Sometimes it is better to be kind than it is to be right. This is the most important lesson I could ever hope to teach you.
—*Love, Mama.*

REFERENCES

Brodkey, L. (1987). Writing ethnographic narratives. *Writing Communication, 4,* 25–50.

Brookes, A. L. (1992). *Feminist pedagogy: An autobiographical approach.* Halifax: Fernwood Publishing.

Chaudhry, L. (2000). Researching "my people," researching myself: Fragments of a reflexive tale. In E. St. Pierre & W. Pillow (Eds.), *Working the ruins: Feminist poststructural theory and methods in education* (pp. 96–113). New York: Routledge.

Collins, P. H. (1991). *Black feminist thought: Knowledge, consciousness, and the politics of empowerment.* New York: Routledge.

Davies, B. (2000). *A body of writing: 1990–1999.* Walnut Creek, CA: AltaMira Press.

Dehli, K. (1991). Leaving the comfort of home: Working through feminisms. In H. Banjeri et. al. (Eds.), *Unsettling relations: The university as a site of feminist struggles* (pp. 45–65). Toronto: Women's Press.

Fine, M. (1992). *Disruptive voices: The possibilities of feminist research.* Ann Arbor, MI: University of Michigan Press.

hooks, b. (2000). *Feminism is for everybody: Passionate politics.* Cambridge, MA: South End Press.

hooks, b. (2003). *Teaching community: A pedagogy of hope.* New York: Routledge.

Luttrell, W. (1997). *Schoolsmart and motherwise: Working class women's identity and schooling.* New York: Routledge.

Maduro, E. S. (2002). Excuse me while I explode: My mother, myself, my anger. In C. Hanauer (Ed.), *The bitch in the house: 26 women tell the truth about sex, solitude, work, motherhood, and marriage* (pp. 3–14). New York: HarperCollins.

McWilliam, E. (2000). Laughing within reason: On pleasure, women, and academic performance. In E. St. Pierre & W. Pillow (Eds.), *Working the ruins: Feminist poststructural theory and methods in education* (pp. 164–178). New York: Routledge.

New International Bible. (1984). Colorado Springs, CO: International Bible Society.

St. Pierre, E. (2000). Nomadic inquiry in the smooth spaces of the field: A preface. In E. St. Pierre & W. Pillow (Eds.), *Working the ruins: Feminist poststructural theory and methods in education* (pp. 258–276). New York: Routledge.

Walkerdine, V. (1986). Post-stimulated theory and everyday social practices: The family and the school. In S. Wilkinson (Ed.), *Feminist social psychology: Developing theory and practice* (pp. 57–76). Philadelphia, PA: Open University Press.

7 A Generation Makes a Difference
The Impact of Family Values on a First- and Second- Generation College-Going Mother and Daughter

Joan Marie Giampa and
Giovanna Bargh Fini

This chapter will focus on how family values shaped the parallel lives of a mother and daughter and their first- and second-generation college experiences.

A FIRST-GENERATION COLLEGE STUDENT THIRTY YEARS LATER

My thirty-year journey into higher education began in the fall of 1978. I applied for one college on a whim earlier that spring because all my friends were going away to college. I was surprised to get an acceptance letter in the mail. My heart raced when I read it, and I began to dream about a new life ahead of me. I remember thinking that I was going to change my destiny and raise myself out of the blue-collar world where I grew up. I worked two jobs that summer and saved $1500 for college. I was off to Shepherd College and my dream of a new and better life began.

Thirty-one years later, I am finishing a doctorate degree in higher education alongside my twenty-two year old daughter, who is graduating from college this spring as a second and third (mother, father) generation college student. Even though our journeys diverged, our family values tied us together.

JOAN'S STORY

If a woman artist has no children, she exempts herself from their demands and has only to underwrite her own goals, so a reasonable variation of the traditional male pattern is available to her . . . On balance; I have logically to welcome whatever life brings my children. Truitt (1996), p. 62–63

My thirty-year journey into higher education and teaching began in the fall of 1978. I applied to one college on a whim earlier that winter to comfort my restless spirit. It seemed like a good idea at the time, since most of my friends were planning to go away to college that fall. I was surprised to get an acceptance letter in the mail from Shepherd College. My heart raced when reading it as I began to dream about life as a college student far removed from my chaotic home life. Home was not a place of refuge due to the influx of new children from age eleven to age seventeen. I remember thinking to myself that I was going to change my destiny and raise myself out of the blue-collar world where I grew up. I bought a pair of cowboy boots that summer before going away to college. In reflection, those cowboy boots were a metaphor of my feelings at the time of stepping into the world of academia. I was a loner and as such, the boots were my way of expressing my individuality and lack of conformity. The cowboy boots also reflected a part of my personality that enjoyed adventure, exploration and rowdiness.

Growing up in an Italian-American family is akin to watching an episode of the popular television series *The Sopranos*. My life was filled with drama, celebration, hard work and plenty of passion. I was born in Arlington, Virginia in 1960. Life in my home was never dull. We had plenty of food on the table, lively dinner interactions, and open displays of affection and love towards one another. We worked hard for the lifestyle we were surrounded by in northern Virginia in the early seventies. During those years between fourteen and seventeen, I worked as a waitress to get the extras that my family could not afford such as cars, clothing and entertainment. I valued my family, friends, loyalty, and my art.

In 1972, we moved to Vienna, Virginia. We lived in the older section of town. This part of Vienna was blue collar and the houses were older ramblers built in the early fifties. Most of the families in this section of Vienna were working class. I always felt I did not belong there. I was embarrassed about where we lived, and a seed was planted during that time to better myself. I have a different lens because those years defined me and my work ethic which carried me through a doctorate program of studies. I cannot afford a house on my old block because they have been torn down and replaced with million dollar homes. Times have changed-even my neighborhood!

Growing up, I had no educational support because my parents were too busy trying to make a living and raising three younger siblings. I learned to memorize schoolwork in class and did not study after school because there was no designated area for studying in my house and the kitchen was too noisy. My parents were more concerned that I do my "job" (which was an unlimited amount of chores) than go to school. When I had a project to complete, I did it without help or supervision, and I learned how to get things done during the school day. I also learned not to ask for help. My mother would always say "Look it up."

My parents did not value education as a means to an end. When I informed my mother I was planning on attending college, she told me that they would not give me any money for college. If they had any extra money, they would give it to my older brother, because he was going to be a bread winner.

These difficult years taught me about self-motivation and responsibility. While most kids were hanging out with their friends and doing after school activities, I was doing chores, working, or helping my mother with my three younger siblings. When I was fourteen, I got a job waiting tables at Bob's Big Boy to fund my teenage lifestyle described earlier. My job at Bob's was the first of over fifty jobs in the restaurant industry that supported me throughout high school, during college, and after college. As it turned out, the early eighties were not the best time to look for a job in graphic design.

I attended Shepherd College for two years before I transferred to James Madison University in the winter of 1980. I graduated in 1983 with a BFA in graphic design. The day before graduation, the art department had a final meeting. I will never forget what the dean of the college suggested to a whole room of BA and BFA's in graduating with an art degree that day. The dean said to "go to work for free, and do anything you can to get in the door" not what I wanted to hear after five long years of college. It certainly foreshadowed what was to come over the next thirty years facing the art world.

When I was a design student, the personal computer did not exist, and we designed everything by hand. Just imagine having to create a headline of type for a layout by shooting light through a metal plate onto photo paper and then developing the headline in a darkroom. We had to wait for the photo paper to dry before we could cut and paste it down to our compositions. It took hours to do then, what it takes seconds to type on a keyboard today. Consequently, when Aldus PageMaker released desktop publishing software and changed the world of page layout in the late 1980's, I was seduced by the medium of computers. I could produce a font, drawing or photograph on paper with a single keystroke. Tasks that used to take days could now be accomplished in minutes. No longer did layouts require intensive labor. With no more Haber rulers, or typesetting machines, or all the people an artist had to deal with in order to get a layout approved for production, the graphic design field was wholly transformed. Design became computerized, and the age of computer graphics emerged.

In 1986, I married David Bargh. David came from a highly educated family and he is a second generation college student. We had two children, Giovanna and Jeremy. By the time I was 32, I was a full-time mom working on my painting career with a home-based carpet cleaning business. David and I decided that a home based business was the best way to raise children and give us the freedom we both sought in our daily schedules. Fibercare Specialists was our business for ten years and it served us well. I did all the marketing, sales and administrative work and David cleaned carpets. I was home with the children and so was he. I could develop my studio work, raise children and manage a small business.

The computer arrived into my household very shortly after my daughter Giovanna was born in 1987, and David developed a database program for our business. Giovanna grew up with all the latest computer technologies. During the early years of her life, she observed her mother operating a home-based graphic design business. The computer became a tool for my design work, and Giovanna grew up watching me grow and develop as a computer artist. The computer parallels our career choice and our lives in this way.

Giovanna graduated from George Mason University in the spring of 2010. Giovanna is as a second/third generation college student. Like her mother, Giovanna will graduate with a BFA in graphic design. Our journeys are similar yet divergent in that she grew up in the world of computers. Our lives have paralleled and our careers are similar yet our family values and traditions tie us together. Giovanna is the digital native and I am the digital immigrant. She has immersed herself in her Italian American roots, while I have ignored my Italian heritage.

The years I spent at home with small children were a great way to live vicariously through them and have a second childhood. Through my children I was able to do the things with them that I did not get to do as a child such as go to museums and spend days at the park. I could teach them to paint and draw and spend time nurturing them. I introduced them to son cultural activities that my parents were not vested in. I was determined to raise my children as well rounded individuals. My children had chores, but their chores had a beginning and an end. Children in Giovanna's generation grew up in a world that invented new and fun things for children to do. It was a time when people were large consumers, when Price Club was our favorite place to shop. My children were privy to all the newest technologies, games, videos, and packaged snacks. Their childhood was a festive time when we had plenty of money to spend. We had the most up-to-date versions of anything we could consume, including computers, games, TV's, videos, and music. Giovanna generation was born in a world where goods were being marketed to and manufactured for children by the "baby boomer" generation. The children of Giovanna's generation are known as the net-generation. The net generation spent many hours alone, using technology as their communication tool. Peer encounters may be by text, instant messaging or social networking sites.

The net-generation comes from a group of predominantly affluent baby-boomer parents, who worked hard to give their children the "best of everything" through enhanced personal development, art and sports training. The net-generation had a closely scheduled activity calendar, leaving little time for personal and social development outside of their day to day schedules. The net-generation is close to their parents as a result of the parental structuring of activities and because of this, net parents feel a sense of ownership over their children's futures.

Since net-generation children's lives were highly structured, they tend to see the world as a place for being involved and planning ahead. Most are very close to their parents and have good relationships with family. Family time is a valuable to them. Therefore, this is where my daughter and I are most alike. For me, college allowed me to break away from my parents. Giovanna never had to flee from me. She actually lived at home for the majority of her college years.

The knowledge I learned as a first generation college student was passed on to my daughter. For example, the college experience is wrought with difficulties. I talked to her about the challenges students face with an over excessive social life in college. I helped her to be a good researcher and artist based on my working knowledge of the college campus. The values she learned at home about hard work and responsibility give her the tools to navigate through life. I have spent most of my life trying to be an accomplished artist and teacher and have accomplished a great deal. I am educated beyond most people in my life and family and continue to improve myself in every area of my life. My daughter is also educated and has been this same strong work ethic.

It is my hope that she passes on what she has learned from me onto the generations to come and to help those that are less fortunate find meaning and passion in their lives through her example and her education. She is a beautiful person who is responsible, compassionate, and motivated to be a productive citizen and a second-generation college graduate.

GIOVANNA'S STORY

I do not think it is uncommon for children to follow the path of their parents. I followed my mothers in terms of my education and I chose the same degree as she. My parents both worked hard to give my brother and me everything we wanted. My generation of kids who grew up in the in the 90s was really spoiled. We always had chores, but we still had time to be kids.

My mother is an artist, and I grew up watching her paint in her studio and was always surrounded by art. I knew she worked very hard to keep up with her artwork, family, job, and school. She went back to graduate school in her late thirties to become a college professor. She is now working towards completing her doctorate in higher education. When my mom went back to school, I remember a frenzy of paintings. She would paint in her studio for hours at a time. Even though she was busy with her schoolwork, she and my dad still signed us up for any activity we wanted, from sports, to dance classes, to music lessons.

I was always a stubborn child. I remember painting with my mom in the studio, where I often felt frustrated with her trying to give me guidance. I had become obsessed with my so-called "smoosh paintings" that my art teacher had us do at school, where we poured different paints onto paper, folded the paper in half, and opened the paper to see that all the paints had mixed together. My mom wanted me to focus on shape and form and to use a paint brush. One day. I announced that I would not be painting with her anymore. Ever since that day, I have regretted my decision. I like to imagine sometimes how my work would have been different had I kept up painting from my childhood. When it came to homework or projects, if I needed help my parents were always there. I usually preferred to do things myself and wanted to be more independent, but that is just my personality. When I was older computer technology rapidly developed and influenced how I was as a student. The Internet affected how I studied: If I couldn't find what I was looking for online, I loathed having to search through at a book instead.

Growing up, I always assumed I would go to college. Both my parents did, and where I grew up in Northern Virginia, people went to college. In school, our teachers told us to stay in school and go to college, because you'll have a better life. When I was in high school and it came time to apply to college, I had no notion of what I wanted to study and no real drive to go away from home. I felt burned out and lazy. This golden opportunity and I was taking it for granted.

Once my friends started getting their acceptance letters and I wasn't, reality gave me a hard slap. I realized that I had wasted my time with my social life my last year and should have applied myself more. I got into a few schools around the state but decided that they were not for me, that I wanted to go to George Mason to be near home and family. Instead of moving away, I decided to go to community college, and after a semester of straight A's, I reapplied and was accepted to George Mason.

I think it was wise for me to spend that semester at community college because it helped me get my priorities straight and think about what I wanted to study. I was torn between three or four majors and could not choose, but I knew I needed to pick something. I knew I liked to be creative, but I also wanted job security in the future. Since George Mason University had a growing Graphic Design department, I chose graphic design as my major. My mom even encouraged me to stay longer at community college because I was doing well and enjoyed it. But, like with my smoosh painting, I wanted to do what I wanted to do, so I went to Mason.

I have heard my mom tell me countless times about her college experience and how it was different from mine. I could not relate to her stories about tracing fonts by hand or how long it took to produce mock-ups. On the simplest level, I could not relate to my mother ever having studied graphic design, since I was so used to her painting. Unlike my mother, I did not have to work to support myself. Although we were not a blue-collar family, we were not rich either. I knew I could not go out of state but that was fine with me. I wanted to be near my family. I didn't want to go to college to party for four years. I wanted to get something out of it.

Since I lived at home while going to college, I was with my mom when she went back to school again, this time for her doctorate. I felt like I had gone back in time ten years to when I was a kid and she was earning her MFA. She was working all the time, and now she had two other children to contend with. However, just like when I was little, she still found time to help me with something I wasn't sure about in my school studies or with my art work. I liked talking with her about art history because of her vast knowledge, and I liked her critiques of the projects I was working on.

When I started college, my dad—who was paying for it—told me I could live on campus or study abroad. My mom told me that if I lived at home she would make sure I got a chance to study abroad. She wanted me to attend community college for several years and then transfer to a four-year school. Because she was a community college teacher, she saw the benefits of a community college education. She felt the teachers were more hands-on with the students. Community college was also less expensive than four year college and I could get my general studies out of the way. Most of the classes were in the evening which allowed me to work during the day.

I loved my Italian heritage and really wanted to study in Italy. I was given the opportunity to go twice, one for language classes and another for a semester abroad. In Italy, I studied printmaking, painting, art history, and graphic design. When I think of my mom I doubt she ever dreamed of studying abroad. It was hard enough just to get by. She worked her way through college and graduate school.

During my four years at George Mason, the art department went through many changes because it moved to a brand new building. For me this improved the art community and I hope will continue to strengthen it. We had brand new computer labs with huge, top-of-the-line Macintosh computers. Everyone was excited about working in such an amazing facility as opposed to the old out-moded equipment and small studio rooms. It was also funny at times to run into my mom when she would go to her classes. It was a unique part of my college experience.

When I was in art school, I went through different changes in my personality. Constant critiques of my work took a mental toll on me. I felt like I was failing all the time and constantly compared myself to others. I really think it has to do with my generation; we were praised for everything we did so it was hard to take criticism. I started to doubt myself and wondered if this was the major for me. I stuck it out, and I finally learned to accept criticism in a healthy way. I began to understand that it was to help me grow as an artist. It also helped me to stop comparing myself so much to others around me. I actually like feedback on my work now because I want to keep improving.

I feel that my college journey was more of a personal struggle of acceptance. I wanted to be good at my work and always tried to do better. With my mom her struggle was to better her life. She never compared herself to others and thought I was being too hard on myself when I told her how I felt. I have grown up in the ME generation, and she grew up where everything was just a struggle—two totally different worlds. I feel very lucky in the sense that I get to actually do something I dreamed about since I was a child. Not a lot of people can say that. My parents paved the way for me to accomplish my dream.

I expected I would have a job after college, but with the war economy being what it is, it is difficult for everyone. Jobs are hard to come by. I was very lucky to gain an awesome internship after college and learned a lot while there. I enjoyed my internship because we were the design department but there was a lot going on and different subject matter to design for. I also do freelance projects on the side to have different pieces to add to my portfolio.

I have become more open-minded about the types of jobs I would want to pursue with this degree. Graphic Design is about thinking and problem-solving, which one must do in any job. I am interested in working in a department of creatives but not necessarily a studio. I like working with a variety of clients because I always learn something new. I am hopeful for my future and the future of this field. It is always changing and evolving, and I am so happy to be a part of it.

One difference between my mother and I, is how we view our Italian heritage. I always embraced it and was proud of my past, while my mother was not. I studied in Italy twice, and it was a dream of mine to be able to live there one day. I studied Italian in college and now have the opportunity to live there. It is an interesting change, whereas my grandparents came here to America, I am returning. I will be getting married to an Italian and starting my life in Venice, Italy.

REFERENCES

Truitt, A. (1996). *Prospect: The journal of an artist.* New York, NY: Penguin Group.

8 Mother May I?

A Daughter of a Low-Income, First-Generation, Single-Parent Household Goes to College

Sinitra N. Johnson

Mother May I is a game that I often played as a child with my friends in Laurens, South Carolina. In the game, before you can make a movement forward, you must ask, "Mother May I?" In the game, "Mother" is a player positioned at one end of the room while the other players are on the opposite end of the room. The goal is to get to where "Mother" is. Sometimes in the game, the "Mother" may not grant your request to move beyond your current location or might even make you take a step backwards. As a player, you constantly are hoping that when you ask, "Mother May I?" the answer will be, "Yes You May." The principles of this game were very present in my life—beyond the playground. My mother was a single, low-income parent with just a high school diploma. She took the game of guiding and nurturing her children very seriously. But she always pushed us forward. I can't recall a time when she asked me to take a step backwards in life or when she prevented me from moving forward.

My mother was raised in rural upstate South Carolina by her maternal grandparents who were born in the South in the early 1900s. Her biological parents died when she was a very young child. My grandparents had a limited education and neither even graduated from high school. My grandfather was a Baptist minister and brick mason. My grandmother was a beautician. My mother grew up most days spending a lot of time in a church and surrounded by elders in the community. Although my grandparents did not have a formal education, they emphasized an education to their children and my mother. My mother did complete 1 year of college at an in-state Historically Black College and University (HBCU). Although she didn't finish, she still firmly believed in the values of God, faith, family, and education that were instilled in her by my grandparents. She has in turn passed these values on to my brothers and me.

Such was the case when it came time to go to college. Once again, I found myself playing this game of permission asking my mother, "Can I go to college?" "Can I take this step forward?" "Am I smart enough to go to college?" My mother's answer was always, "Yes—you can do anything." But that's just it, she always encouraged and supported me to continue my education after high school, yet we had no real conversations on what it took to actually be admitted to college or the preparation that was involved. It was not because she did not care; she simply did not know the process. Although, I had two older brothers who entered college before me, my mother still did not fully understand things such as choosing a major, the college admissions process, financial aid, or all of the paperwork that was required for me to begin my studies at a university. She just knew that she wanted me there. I can remember taking four college applications home from school. I visited three colleges for a campus tour and attended one admissions night event. But I decided to apply to only two colleges. My first selection was based merely on the fact that the college had the words "University" and "South Carolina" in the name (*University* because that meant college to me and *South Carolina* because that meant in-state tuition). I applied to the second school simply because my high school friends applied. I never looked at things such as the location, the size of the student body, majors offered, academic support programs, tuition and fees, or student-to-teacher ratio. I never developed an alternative educational plan that I could rely on in the event that I was not admitted to one of the two colleges where I submitted applications. I never considered if my financial aid would cover the cost of my tuition and fees. Nor did I even think or know the impact of using student loans to pay for my expenses. Once I got to college I continued to make uninformed decisions. When it was time to select a major, I chose criminal justice. I didn't choose this major because I had a passion for it or I exhibited potential in it. I chose it because social work, which was my first choice, was not a major offered. I attended a summer program sponsored by the College of Criminal Justice, so without a rhyme or reason, criminal justice became my major of study. I did not sit down with anyone to discuss my strengths, weaknesses, likes, dislikes, or my career plan. I did not take a Myer-Briggs inventory or other career interest surveys.

So, there I was, a first-generation, low-income (FG/LI) college student admitted to a flagship university and immediately lost. Getting into college presented challenges. Staying in college required navigating many road-blocks that had been placed in my path long before I moved onto campus. These other barriers included my poor preparation in secondary school, lack of computer skills, being a minority student at a large predominantly white institution, and just not fitting in with the student body. The shock of not having "Mother" for permission to move forward and take the next step was quite intimidating for me.

I often wonder if I were not a first-generation, low-income student, would this transition have been different? The transition for me was not about being homesick nor did I feel loneliness because I was away from home. My mother's values and skills of independence emerged for me living in a residence hall with no parental supervision. I rarely went to parties on "school nights" or came out of my room before I finished my homework because these had always been my mother's rules. I was able to get up for 8 a.m. classes, rarely oversleeping. I balanced school, free time, and my social life. My transition and insecurities had more to do with policies and politics of a college campus. Within my first semester, I learned that my financial aid award was not available because I waited until June to submit the financial aid application. My mother and I waited until June because I thought I needed to pay for my residence hall application fees first. The college process was a maze and we were just hoping we were making the right turns. On the academic front, I was being newly exposed to skill sets that many of my peers saw as basic—sending an e-mail, obtaining articles on microfilm, writing papers in APA style, and using the Internet. All of these were firsts for me. I had never done these things before in my life.

Despite all of this, my first semester was successful. I had over a 3.5 GPA and was invited into the Freshman Honor Society. My mother was so proud. She has always supported me inside and outside of the classroom. It never ended. In high school I could always count on her being in the audience for me no matter how small my part or role was in a performance. It did not matter if I got "playing time" or if I was on the bench for the entire game, she was there. One of my fondest memories of my mother and grandmother showing me support was when they traveled to USC for the freshman honor society induction ceremony. It was at this moment, that I think my entire childhood flashed before me. It was at this moment that I realized the important role that my family had played in my life. Here I was in college, many miles away from home, but my mom was still coming to show her support like it was a PTA meeting down the street—just to say "I am proud of you Sinitra."

However, I still had this feeling of not belonging at the university. During winter break, I shared with my mother that after my freshman year, I wanted to transfer to the state supported Historically Black College. I just did not fit in where I was and wanted to feel like I was in the right place. My mother, granted me permission to move forward with the transfer, but only after I completed the entire year and gave it a little more time. For the first time, when I asked, "Mother May I?" the answer was "No . . . stand still." At the beginning of my second semester, I was introduced to a federal TRIO program that assisted students like me. When I met with the counselor for the program, he informed me that I was not previously selected as a participant because of the late submission of my financial aid application. He accepted me into the program, gave me one-on-one advisement, and placed me into a cohort of classes with other students that shared similar backgrounds. Finally, I was in a community where I felt like others reflected me. In this program, there were other FG/LI students; there were other students who needed tutoring, mentoring, and study skill development outside of the classroom; there were other students who needed to attend cultural events and programs; there were other students who came from a single-parent home. There were students like me. And so, because my mother so wisely ordered me to stand still, I found myself standing in the right place when OSP came to greet me (Opportunity Scholars Program is a federal TRIO program funded under a Student Support Services grant). This program took over in guiding me where my mother was not able to help. In many ways, it became a "second mom"—a second parent that helped me step by step through my college experience. I would always ask my OSP advisors before I considered moving forward or taking another step that impacted my education. It was also my OSP counselor who placed a book in my hand about going to graduate school and obtaining a master's degree.

These experiences happened in my first year of college and shine a light on the challenges faced by students like me. Parental *support* is not all that is needed for low-income, first-generation college students to prepare and successfully graduate from college. Students and parents need an education on how to navigate college. Ultimately, it was my own college experience that shaped my decision to assist first generation, low-income college students with access to higher education as a career. I now serve as the director of another TRIP program, Upward Bound, at a community-based college in South Carolina. Access must go beyond just assisting students with submitting the college application or providing a waiver for a standardized test during the junior and senior years. Institutions that admit first-generation, low-income students must understand what barriers and other issues students are bringing to their college experience. Universities must understand the importance that families play in a student's success. In developing support programs that focus on the success, retention, and graduation of students, parental education and involvement must be included. Often parents are invited on campus for college tours, orientations, and parent weekends during football seasons. But what information is provided directly to the parent? We often use these events as a first step in trying to "cut the cord" between students and their parents. This surface level involvement is just a glimpse of the experience to come. Students learn that their parent can no longer obtain their academic record without their permission. Parents can no longer call to ask a counselor or teacher how their students are progressing. Parents can simply visit, "enjoy" campus, and offer support from a distance. It is very important for a student to gain independence. However, students who are first-generation may not know how to maneuver this maze. Everyone must be involved in helping—on campus and at home. Below I share my concept for such a holistic framework. It is based on many years working professionally with first-generation college students and having been one myself. Assisting this population must include:

TRAIN THE TRAINER

I am reminded of the bible verse, "Direct your child into the right path, and when they are older, they will not leave it." Higher education professionals must train and prepare the "trainer"—families. Universities and parents can become partners in a student's success. Admissions marketing strategies should target mailings for parents of first-generation, low-income students that address challenges and barriers often faced by these students.

Inform parents how they can play a role in their child's success. Make parents aware of on-campus support services for their child. During parent weekend and orientation sessions, offer engaging and interactive sessions for parents to educate them on the college admission process and on college life. This means using these sessions as "teaching moments," not simply presenting and talking at parents. Make it a workshop or training session.

CASE MANAGEMENT

College personnel must understand what other barriers exist beyond the family income and educational level of parents. My college counselors or faculty never knew that as a student, I struggled with writing and spelling or that I had behavioral problems for many years. They never knew that as a middle school student, my art teacher told me that I would work at McDonald's when I graduated from high school. We must begin to know and understand the whole student and his or her full experience. An advisor or college counselor who knows about a student's upbringing can better understand how to serve him or her in the present situation. A counselor can then examine what a student's values and belief systems are and have an understanding of how and why he or she makes certain decisions. The case management approach allows university officials to chart a student's entire development each year. They can examine a student's academic, social, and emotional development. This system will also allow universities the opportunity to have longitudinal data of barriers from real life students. There may be some merit to combining my initial interest in social work with my current passion for college student success.

TUTORING AND MENTORING

Often this population cannot receive assistance from parents in advanced course work due to the parent's academic capacity. Or the parent may not be available to give advice on critical homework because of demanding work obligations. So, students should be aligned with a mentor from a similar background to help them move forward. A professional mentor or a faculty mentor can be very important. Many frameworks for mentoring programs are for a student's freshman year only. A better format would be to extend the mentoring relationship throughout all 4 years at the university.

FINANCIAL AID COUNSELING AND FINANCIAL LITERACY

Students and parents must be counseled on the importance of completing financial aid forms early and on time. Additionally, the counseling should include student loan advising beyond the online entrance counseling. It is imperative that FG/LI students know the financial responsibility they are taking on when they take out student loans. My overage in student loans financed my trips to the mall each semester and also allowed me to send money back home to my mother to assist with her bills. I saw the money as free money. I had no true understanding that I would one day have to repay my student loans. Also, I saw my mother struggle financially and she could not send me money each month so the money was a part of my survival at college. Students must know the true sticker price for their degrees. After graduating from college, the salaries offered by entry-level jobs were in the low $20,000s. I thought the degree meant instant access to the middle class—another misconception.

CAREER PLANNING

Deciding a career is one of the biggest decisions students will make. FG/ LI students must be exposed to job shadowing, career interest inventories, and real life professionals in their desired professions. Additionally, salary projections should be examined for the area where they desire to live. When I left my mother's house in the mid 1990s, I left with the career goal of becoming a juvenile social worker. I am doing something that is much different and a much better fit. Before coming to college, I never knew student services to be a career option. Having gone through much of my college career not knowing my options is the very reason why I decided to make it my life goal to help students achieve their educational goals and successfully navigate college. I want students to know that their current barriers do not block them from moving forward or moving beyond the starting point. There are too many supporters like family, counselors, advisors, and professors available to help them move around it. We are all cheering them on—as a team.

And so now I have the pleasure of assuming the role of "college mother." My students come to me with their hopes and dreams, challenges and frustrations. And when they ask, *"Mother may I, Mother can I, Mother should I move forward?," my* answer is "Yes you may! Go ahead and move forward, just never forget to assist someone else in this game!"

Part III
Fathers

9   Gifts From My Father

Sondra Frank

I am a product of a single-parent household where my mother was the primary caregiver. Although my father had an on-again, off-again presence for many of my adolescent years, I honestly don't have many memories of longing for him when he wasn't around. I never really connected with him fully as a father until last year when I received a call informing me that he was in the hospital with throat cancer and that he might not make it. It had been 16 years since I'd last seen my father but I didn't hesitate to pack my bag and head down south to Alabama where my roots run deep. The days that led up to my arrival were nothing short of disquieting. How would I respond to seeing him after so many years? How would he? Would I even recognize him? So many questions ran through my mind with regards to this news, most of them having to do with why it had to take a tragedy for us to see each other.

This man, who stood 6 feet 5 inches tall and was once a very strong man was now lying in a hospital bed withering away. And even though I spent a better part of my life blaming him for much of my shortcomings, a love that I didn't even know existed rose to the surface. It was genuine. Being there for him didn't feel like a duty, but rather my desired service. To my surprise, although I was angry at the choices he made in his life, the nurturer in me went to work making sure he was cared for, not taken advantage of, that he had an advocate working on his behalf (because he didn't have insurance) and that he was as comfortable as one could be in his situation.

For four months I was back and forth to see him and I can honestly say that my journey to healing began the first day I saw him in his hospital bed and still continues to this day 1 year later. Each time I visited, I would stay for hours and I could tell that his heart was full by my presence. I was his part-time, out-of-town caregiver and the nurses who cared for him on a daily basis were always happy to see me because he allowed me to care for him in a way that he wouldn't allow others. When I arrived, they would always say that they knew I was coming—everyday leading up to my visit he would announce that I was on my way. With each trip, I came bearing gifts, toiletries, PJs, clothes, and skull caps, which were his favorite. We often sat in silence, watching TV, or I would spend the time working to make sure he was comfortable. He couldn't speak well due to the trachea put into his throat, but he always managed to thank me several times throughout the day. Regardless of his communication challenges he would constantly tell me that he was proud of me and that he loved me. This was new for us. I can only recall a handful of times where we actually spoke the words "I love you," but as he was coming to the end of his life it flowed naturally. I wished there had been a sense of urgency to cultivate that relationship while he was healthy. Even though I didn't necessarily feel deprived of love, I believe that love must be actively engaged—speaking as well as showing it is necessary. But what was most shocking to me was the profound effect that his words had on my spirit—having him say that he was proud deeply affected me. I believe in my heart of hearts that had I been told this throughout my youth and even as I matriculated through college it would have made a huge difference. As I reflect back, not knowing or being reassured that what I was doing was right or good left me a bit insecure while I was in school. Teachers and mentors are undoubtedly important but family is everything. I can admit that I have doubted myself a great deal in life. I questioned my purpose often. His support would have helped to affirm and to give even more meaning to my life. But I am happy to know that in the end, I was able to provide him this affirmation instead. Sadly, my father lost his battle with cancer 4 months after being diagnosed, but knowing that he genuinely wanted and needed me there felt more than good, and my heart was full knowing that my presence made a difference in his life.

I've gone through many life experiences that have helped shape what I now believe about my parents. They did the best they could with what they had and what they knew. I often didn't think that their efforts were good enough. But now I realize that out of every circumstance comes a life lesson, and much of the woman that I am and the person that I will become is due largely to my family. With all of the mistakes that were made, I've received many gifts from my father. As I've started on this healing journey, I've come to realize that I've been learning valuable lessons from his life all along. Some are lessons I'm still learning. As I unwrap each of these gifts, I realize that I could never have learned these things in a classroom. Some lessons were learned from the good that my father did. Others were learned as a result of his shortcomings. But all of them have made me a better person.

GIFT #1: GIVE FROM THE HEART

I don't even know if he knew that the gifts he gave weren't really "ordinary" or "regular" gifts, he just gave them. When my father did give gifts, he genuinely gave them from his heart. Unapologetically. I can recall as early as 4 years old waking up on a few occasions to fireball candies under my pillow. On birthdays and or random visits I remember him bringing things like pecans, granny smith apples, pomegranates, and if I was lucky, chocolate kisses. I would even go as far as saying that the long walks and trips to the park were intangible gifts of time. I didn't get those consistently but I got them nonetheless.

Thinking about this brings me a certain level of joy and I know it has had an impact on me. My father's giving spirit has helped me to form my own—he influences the many ways that I give of myself and the many gifts that I now share with people. Just as my dad gave without strings attached, I notice that I tend to do the same. I think this is one of the major things that has made me successful in fostering positive personal and professional relationships over the years. Like my dad, the gifts that I do give aren't always ordinary or tangible gifts, but they are meaningful. Be it a listening ear, a phone call to simply say hello, a handmade card, a smile, a warm welcome, or the gift of presence. I think this is a valuable lesson and tends to be a lost art in a "what's in it for me" society. My dad didn't just show me how to be successful—he showed me how to be a good person.

GIFT #2: NEVER PUT OFF UNTIL TOMORROW WHAT CAN BE DONE TODAY

This is one of those lessons that we had to learn the hard way. My dad left New Jersey (where I grew up) to go back Alabama when I was just about to enter my teenage years. I saw him once when I was in high school, one time while I attended college at Howard University, and then not again until he was on his sick bed, fighting for his life. I was 38. Although he often spoke of needing to visit with my brother, his grandchildren and me, it never amounted to more than just a thought or a desire. Although I did make efforts over the years by sending him pictures of our family, it would have been much more meaningful if he were able to see his children or hug and hold the grandkids. It would have made a difference in our relationship and how I viewed him. His not making the effort led me to believe that seeing us wasn't something that was really important to him. I've now come to understand that it wasn't necessarily intentional—it was simply a subconscious thing that had more to do with some personal demons he battled. I honestly think that one of the things that caused my father to hesitate in visiting us was fear. Fear of rejection. Maybe he was scared because of the uncertainties. Maybe he felt like he never measured up as a father. He was afraid because he knew that he had failed us in a way. Fear is the thing that often will hold us back from doing, going, or being. For my father, the chance to know his grandchildren never came. One of the shortcomings that I learned from my dad was procrastination—putting things off. I believe that this plays a role in my life professionally and personally. As far as relationships, for example, because there are certain issues from my past that I seek to avoid, there are some friends that I intentionally don't call or visit often because I know that our conversations are going to require that I confront past issues. As it relates to my professional life, I find that I delay some of my more challenging assignments out of fear as well, sometimes lacking the confidence that I will do a good job. As I'm becoming increasingly aware of my initial tendency to put things off, be it out of fear or apathy, I can begin to put in place strategies to help me change my behavior. But understanding the role that my family plays as the root of the problem is important. Our behavior does not just come out of nowhere, it is motivated by what we are taught, experience, and observe.

GIFT #3: SEEING THE GOOD IN PEOPLE

For the most part, my father was a loner. But I do specifically remember two people he called friend. Tim and Pedro. They were nice, but I can remember thinking at a young age that these men were a little eccentric. One was a dancer, a substitute teacher in my hometown, and he also worked with my dad as a cook in a hotel. The other, a short Latino man with a squeaky voice, was a friend that my father made while living in a boarding house. I am comfortable saying that both of these men were the complete opposite of my father. As I reflect on this, I don't think my father judged either of these guys by their outward appearance, or by what they did. I truly believe that he looked at their hearts, that he took the time to know them as people as opposed to judging them and missing out on potentially meaningful friendships.

As a child and even in my adult life I think about how I've had and still have the tendency to befriend those who are different from me. I would say all of these friends were simply unique spirits. Not that I haven't been guilty of being judgmental at times, but I, like my father, have this way of being able to see the whole person. Without a doubt I believe this has helped me as I navigated life. I remember in grade school being friends with a girl who had a condition that would cause her to wet her pants often. This caused her to be ostracized by her fellow classmates. I didn't hesitate to become her friend. I can recall several other occasions as a child befriending or simply being nice to those that had been judged by others due to a lack of understanding. What I've learned from my father is to not put people in boxes. Because I grew up in a small town amongst many of the same friends, I saw college as an opportunity to meet many people from varied backgrounds. Because my family has always taught me the value of diversity I was able to more fully appreciate it in college. This has also helped me a great deal in the workplace as I have learned to appreciate people in spite of their differing opinions and personalities. Too often, those that are a bit different are labeled as the problem (in schools, offices, social clubs, etc.). But my dad taught me to dig deeper and to avoid labeling people as weird or wrong and instead to give them the label of friend.

GIFT #4: IT'S OKAY TO ASK FOR HELP

Both my mother and my father are guilty of not asking for help when needed. This has been something that I've personally grappled with all of my life. Being the loner that he was, I can't recall very many times where my father asked others for anything. I believe this has had a significant impact on me. From my adolescent years through college and even now into my adult professional life, I wrestle with asking people for help. Unfortunately, this hard-headedness has often been the difference between just decent grades and academic excellence. Not seeking out help has made the difference between being the good player on the sports team versus the star player. As an adult, my hesitation to receive help has also cost me promotions at work that I know I deserve. If there is one piece of advice I could pass along to anyone it's to ask for help when you need it. I would even encourage parents to teach their children to do so and to cultivate an environment where it's okay to admit that you need help. I am growing through this one every day and it has truly been an uphill battle. Again, he didn't quite get this one right and I unfortunately inherited this bad habit. But even in his errors he showed me the consequences of such actions. Sometimes the negative lesson is priceless.

GIFT #5: LESS IS MORE

If there was anyone that I knew in my life who could live off of very little it was my father. I affectionately used to call him Grizzly Adams and I remember telling people as I grew up that he "lived off the land." I can't with all sincerity recall a time in my life where my father ever had more than he needed. He often stayed in rooming houses where he lived an extremely modest lifestyle. Perhaps that had something to do with his upbringing. He was one of seven boys and so his family didn't have the resources to enjoy excess. Living off little as opposed to more is a lesson that I really need to take from him. I think living this simple life made it easier for him to come and go as he pleased. He was very clean and organized. He never had a lot of clothing, and his toiletries were always packed away neatly in a black leather toiletry bag. Being a music lover his albums were organized neatly by year and by genre. As I look over my own life and examine all the "stuff" that I have acquired over the years, I don't see how these things have ever given me lasting happiness or have even added to my life in meaningful ways. Although I may have looked down on my father at times because of his lifestyle, the reality is that he had it right all along. He didn't need things to validate him as a man nor did he need things to make him happy. On the other hand, being a single parent, my mother had to work hard for everything she gave my brother and me. Although the town where I grew up had a number of affluent and upper middle class families, I didn't experience pressure to have as much as others. People may have had things but they weren't showy. Because there was this what's mine is yours sense of community amongst my peers, I didn't really pay attention to those things that I was without. However, when I entered college at Howard University, which is notoriously known as a fashionably conscious campus, there was a bit of a priority shift. There was a certain pressure, an inner desire to materialistically compete with my peers. But the real pressure actually came as I graduated, moved out on my own, entered the workforce, and began to make money. As I started to interact on a different level with young professionals, I was introduced to this culture of "I gotta get mine" and the desire for more things increased because I felt there was this certain level of entitlement. Now, I'm beginning to take a more in depth look at my father's life and glean from him those things that will help me live a more simple life. Although my father may not have left a financial legacy, the legacy of knowing that less is more and that true happiness is found in the simple things in life is priceless.

GIFT #6: WRITE LETTERS

My father was a letter writer indeed. He wrote me letters off and on for most of my adult years. They all pretty much said similar things, but in an age where technology has taken away the personal touch, it was nice that he actually took the time out to write to me. I have learned over the years the power of this gift. I may not send traditional letters often, but I never send cards without personal notes and I even make handmade cards when time permits. In both school and the workforce it is now essential to embrace e-mail, social networking, and other forms of virtual communication. Institutions have moved us forward in our abilities as communicators, but many of our families gave us the foundation of what meaningful communication and interaction looks like. What I've come to appreciate is that when someone takes the time out of their schedule to write a note of thanks or to let you know that they are thinking of you, it goes a long way. Since I graduated from college 14 years ago, I've been employed with the same organization. The one thing that has set me apart and has played a significant role in the relationships that I've built over the years with coworkers and the countless number of volunteers with whom I work, has been the layered ways in which I communicate. Colleagues old and new still share that they felt welcomed when they started with the organization either because of a note, e-mail, or as a joke, an autographed picture of myself I gave them. Admittedly, I do these things out of sheer joy of making people feel welcome and accepted.

GIFT #7: EVERYTHING IS GOING TO BE ALRIGHT

My father was a peacekeeper. Although he did give himself permission to get angry, he had this amazing ability to not let things bother him—to not sweat the small stuff. He didn't spend countless hours worrying about what people thought of him. If I questioned him about anything his response was always "Oh, everything's gone be alright." It would aggravate me at times. It really frustrated me when he was sick. But the reality is in the end everything does have to be alright. Things may not always work out the way we want but in the end they will always work out the way they need to. We always get through it. Dev Patel said it best in the movie, *The Best Exotic Marigold Hotel*, "everything will be alright in the end and if it's not alright, then it's not the end."

GIFT #8: PRAY EVERY DAY

In his later years my father became a Christian and he ended every phone call and every letter by telling me to pray every day. I think for me this is a valuable and necessary practice. I still have yet to cultivate the discipline of prayer as I occasionally get caught up in the notion of prayer being an exercise in religious duty rather than a simple conversation with my God. My father has motivated me to get to a point where I realize that conversation is not limited to a church, or on my knees, but can include writing letters, daily journaling, sitting in silence, and meditation. Prayer is as much about listening as it is speaking. However I choose to pray, I do agree with my dad, what is important is that I just do it.

GIFT #9: BE YOURSELF

One thing I can say about my father is that he never pretended to be someone he wasn't. What you saw is what you got. Period. To be honest, I don't think he even understood the concept of trying to be someone or something else. He only knew how to be himself and how to embrace the life that was his. Not perfect but authentic. I think this gift in particular is one by which I try to live my life. I believe it is my genuineness that people have come to appreciate. Years ago as a college student and now as a professional, I have definitely had formal experiences that taught me be independent and autonomous. But I have to acknowledge the ways that my family taught me to be an individual, to like who I am, and to walk my own path in life.

THE POINT OF IT ALL

Since my father's passing, I find myself learning more from his life as I go. By no means do I feel like I've mastered anything and unfortunately some of the lessons have come with a hefty personal cost. But what I do know is that in spite of all of his mistakes, setbacks, and shortcomings he continues to help me become a better me every day. Throughout my adolescent years I struggled in many ways not having my dad around. Even throughout college and much of my adult life he was not present. And what I've learned from all of this is the importance of being present. When I say present, I'm not referring to someone just being there or just showing up. For me, I think it's an experience or group of experiences that goes much deeper. You can be a part of someone's life, even when they are far away at college. You can be actively engaged in what is happening with them as they move through new life experiences and environments. I wanted my father's presence while I was in college. I needed his presence as I started life as an adult. One thing that I know very well is disconnection from a family member and it doesn't feel very good. We need our families. So, I value the bits of wisdom that I was able to take from my father. And I let those lessons serve as my guide as I become more of the person that I was meant to be. My dad helped make me a better, more caring person, one who believes strongly in building healthy relationships, one who sees and accepts people for who they are, and one who offers support and encouragement to others. I am also learning the importance of being present in the right now because when you live in the past or future, it becomes very easy to miss out on the freedom that exists at this moment. I get to forgive the past, and embrace the now. I can honestly say that I've come to a place where I not only have found forgiveness in my heart for the choices my father made but I've found a certain freedom that comes along with forgiving. I've finally had that "aha" moment that every teacher dreams of for her students. My dad's lessons weren't perfect—they weren't always grand; sometimes they weren't presented very well; and sometimes the lesson was learned through disappointment. But ultimately I know for sure that his gifts helped me to find my truth and to embrace it. And so like he taught me, I am taking this opportunity to write him a final thank you letter through this book chapter.

10 Piece by Piece
Laying Down the Road Map to Purpose and Agency

Edward J. Smith

PAVING THE PATH: THE UNHEARD TALE OF BLACK FATHERHOOD

> He was one thing many other fathers were not: He was there. Present and accounted for every day. Emotionally absent, mind you. But there, at least, in body. I know so many men, so many black men, who cannot say the same. So many men for whom the absence of a father is a wound that never scabbed over. (Pitts, 1999, p.12)

The tale of black fatherhood is a complex narrative that is rarely accurately told. American popular media and scholarly literature alike use broad brush strokes to paint a picture that illustrates black fathers as irresponsible, emotionally and physically "absent," and, if present, demonstrates them as insensitive and uncaring. Although enduring evidence supports the notion of the non-resident black father (Lerman & Sorensen, 2000; Livingston & Parker, 2011), very rarely does popular discourse discuss the financial and emotionally "present" black fathers, whether in the home or otherwise. Even less often do we hear of the experiences of black single fathers or guardians, for whom engagement and accountability more accurately describe their parenthood posture (Hamer & Marchioro, 2002). As Coles and Green (2009) observe, it's important to note that absence is only one slice of the black fatherhood pie and a much smaller slice than normally portrayed in popular discourse.

As a single man, my father did everything he could to take care of me and rear me with careful guidance, sound ethics, and a motivation that would drive me throughout my formative years. His engagement and support lead me to commit myself to my academic engagements, athletic pursuits, and community service and activism. He started his initial journey through parenthood, subscribing to strict familial gender roles: As a father, he thought it was important to teach me the values of hard work, responsibility, and toughness. After my mother passed away, I started to see a gradual shift in his parenting style; he started instilling in me traits stereotypically facilitated by mothers; he soothed me and supported me through my sorrow, cared for me, taught me how to cook and clean for myself, and eventually, through encouraging me to deepen my interaction with my younger cousins and the elders in my family, he taught me about caregiving and nurturing.

The more I grow, the more I notice (and hope) that I resemble the man I know my father to be. A quiet and discreet man, my father's speech combines the country patois of his Jamaican beginnings, the unpretentiousness of his adult years in Toronto, and the edgy force of his more senior years in northern New Jersey. He is a role model to many and an exemplar of guardianship and accountability. Responsibility is nothing new to him, as he came from a family of 12 brothers and sisters, and was forced to take on a guardian role at the age of 13 when his father died. He then helped rear four younger brothers, who all went on to be upstanding adults and fathers. More than anything, his adolescent experience prepared him for his own experiences with fatherhood. He would eventually watch his wife suffer from sickle cell anemia, struggle to survive, and live most of her life under severe physical duress and persistent stints in the hospital. My mother underwent numerous treatments, blood transfusions, and surgeries, eventually leading to her death. He was forced to rear his 9-year-old son by himself, working two jobs, for most of my childhood, to put forth a strong effort to keep me away from the many elements outside of the home that could lead down an unhealthy and unproductive path.

Although I often made single parenthood challenging for my father, he persevered; he continually strived to be the best caregiver and provider he could be. He often would take on the child care responsibilities of some of my friends and peers. They often looked up to him when we were younger, telling me—consciously or unconsciously—how much they envied my relationship with my father. Some of my friends and cousins didn't have their fathers in their lives; some of them had fathers present, but they didn't experience the tight bond that my father and I shared. As I reflect on experiences with my childhood friends and peers, I can say that I didn't grow up knowing or seeing another father–son relationship—or another father—like my own. For that, I will be eternally grateful and fortunate, and our love for each other will continue to grow as our lives continue to unfold. But it was a critical period between completing my college degree and starting a new life as a professional when my appreciation for my father became even clearer.

NAVIGATING VALUES AND WORK PRODUCT: MAKING A LIVING OR LIVING A LIFE

I cried tears of joy on the night of my graduation ceremony. Although the dinner tables, arranged adjacently, were surrounded by 17 of my closest and most famished family members and friends, I was fixated on my father's eyes. It was at that moment that I felt like I was becoming everything he wanted me to be. The numerous sacrifices and the opportunities forgone were finally paying off. We had taken this journey to and through higher education, together, step-by-step, in support of building a better life for me—for us.

It was only fitting that I seized the opportunity to publically acknowledge him in front of my dinner party and anyone else in the restaurant who would listen. This bachelor's degree in economics was not only earned by my intellectual and emotional faculties, but by those who, although they missed this particular road, left footprints, signs, and signals to blaze a trail. With the lights dimmed, I instructed the entire restaurant to shine an imaginary spotlight on my father and acknowledge that he, through challenge and triumph, did the right thing. Responsible and accountable, he reared me, by himself, and as much as we were convened to celebrate my accomplishment, we should be celebrating his invariable display of excellent fatherhood. I was now a college graduate, embarking on a journey that would lead me to take a position with a large international investment bank as an analyst working with corporations, governments, and high net worth clients around the world. But even more, I was poised to continue to make my father proud.

Nine months later, I was deep into the trenches of being a new professional. The long days and even longer nights of booking trades, processing investment and redemption agreements, and dealing with the insatiable fiscal appetite of pompous, self-absorbed, and voracious clients and colleagues took its toll on my mind, body, and spirit. As the days blended into weeks, and the weeks blended into months, I often wondered where this path would lead me. My discontent was motivated by several factors. First, I knew most of my work peers, particularly those in my age bracket, did not come from my same socioeconomic background. I had to cross a number of roadblocks and speed bumps to get to the seat next to them on the trading desk, impediments that many were unfamiliar with and had no cultural context to learn about. I knew their experience and in many ways had to embrace their ways of knowing and being, but they did not have to know mine—it didn't matter. I saw numerous colleagues in the early 40s suffer heart attacks. I saw drug use for simple human activities that should come naturally—things like going to sleep, waking up, or just to have a pleasant attitude throughout the day. These were folks in their 30s. Worst of all, I saw my values and principles tested daily by the wicked undercurrents of racism, sexism, capitalism, and the systematic exploitation of the marginalized and disenfranchised. Yes, I had a serious chip on my shoulder.

These feelings were juxtaposed with my experiences when I returned home. Night after night—or rather morning after morning—I'd return home to my father, so proud that I'd secured and excelled in such a challenging and seemingly sophisticated job. He was proud of the lucrative financial rewards that came with this job. But of course he was. Things like good salaries are so subtly and obviously alluring to anyone coming from a community where money—and the need to have more of it—consistently occupied our thoughts. And although money certainly wasn't everything to us, not having it, at times, felt like it was everything. I would be able to contribute to the family and not only "pay it forward" but "pay it back" by contributing to the daily upkeep of our home. Perhaps I didn't see it as a sacrifice. Although I wasn't happy and I wasn't soulfully fulfilled, my desire to see my father and family supported outweighed my desire to spend most of my time thinking of ways to advance humanity. Nevertheless, I would always rationalize my decision and continued participation by saying that I was working for the two of us—my dad and me. But yet, as I strived to achieve professional excellence, I began to feel like I was drifting steadily away from the man I was once so close to.

Soon thereafter, I was confronted with the reality that, emotionally, I was running out of steam and my heart just couldn't take the type of unfulfilling life in which I was now fully entrenched. With each new work day I was becoming implicated—directly or indirectly—in a discrete set of investments, decisions, and actions that were in stark opposition to the very values taught by my family and educational mentors. Although I thought I was working for them, the work I was doing was actually working against who my family was—who I was. Throughout my time as an undergraduate student, I had been vigorously active in student organizations and clubs that advanced the campus's collective consciousness of cultural awareness and sensitivity. Whether it was leading campus initiatives to increase multicultural programming or working with campus leadership to organize sit-ins, protests, press conferences, and rallies, advocating for equity and empowerment with respect to race, gender, and sexual identity, I frequently engaged in social and communal activism, and observed Dr. Martin Luther King's philosophy of servant leadership, which at times led me straight to the halls of the senior leadership of our university's administration, advocating for safe and healthy environments for all of our minoritized and marginalized groups. I also led mentoring organizations and coordinated service learning experiences by traveling to our nearest urban centers to learn from community organizers in their respective fields as they strived to improve the quality of life for their fellow community members. I even spent time living in these communities hoping to lend my intellectual and physical capabilities to their efforts. In college, I learned a lot about life, work, and struggle. Perhaps it wasn't about the proverbial "making a difference"; more so, it was about identifying the needs and desires of those in my community and submitting to a movement that was greater than, or outside of, my own lived experience. Throughout it all, I always thought about my father, and how proud he was of all that I was doing during my undergraduate career. While wrestling with this perceived dichotomy, I received a call on a balmy spring afternoon from my father that changed my perspective on life and work, and eventually, brought the both of them together for me.

THE DARK OF THE TUNNEL: FIGHTING THE GOOD FIGHT

The economic downturn between 2008 and 2011 had a disastrous effect on job prospects and overall financial stability for everyone, particularly black men (Austin, 2009; Austin, 2010; Tsoi-A-Fatt, 2010; Pew Center for Research, 2010). It made me think of the old adage: When it rains hard, everybody gets wet, at least a little bit. But as the research suggests, it has appeared that some experienced a downpour and were drowning in economic struggle.

It was about 3 p.m. on a balmy April day when I received a phone call at my desk while at work. It was my father, telling me he had received instructions to collect his personal items from his work station and to exit the company premises. He had the rest of the day to tell everyone goodbye and would have the next morning to collect any large personal items or equipment that he couldn't take home that day. He was let go. It was as if his lifeline of support was in somebody else's hands, and that person simply let go of it. There was no tremor in his voice—no tears, no sobs. It was something he saw coming, nonetheless, the news still hit him—hit us—like a box cutter under the jaw. I abruptly ended my workday, collected my items, and immediately left my office to find him. I didn't know what I would do or tell him when I found him. I was enraged that his company would let him go after 20 years of service. This was a man who had worked his way from the supply room to the mail room to office work. For all the striving he had done, they let him go without a second thought and he was left to fend for himself.

Throughout the next 4 years, I would see my father struggle to maintain employment, temporary or permanent, part-time or full-time. As confident and upbeat as he was, in private, it began to take its toll on him—on us. In my observations extending outside of my father's experience and into my town, my neighborhood, and my community, I learned a few devastating realities about the socio-emotional impacts of unemployment. Not only does unemployment take a toll on the unemployed, but it imposes pain and distress on the loved ones and communities in its midst. Prolonged unemployment can rupture emotions and permanently damage psyches, self-concept and self-worth in particular. One of the most painful impacts of prolonged unemployment, however, is that it makes you second guess most, if not all, of the positive decisions you've made in your life. This is especially painful when you think you've played the game fairly and you just couldn't secure a win for your team.

As the son of a 53-year-old man with no college degree who worked temporary appointments totaling 15 months in 4 years, and a woman for whom employment (whether gainful or not) was always contingent on her sporadic physical health, I've become very clear about the very painful realities of unemployment (both familial and communal). Although this was painful at the time, it all changed on another spring afternoon when my father received a call from Factory Five Racing, Inc. That was the genesis of my newfound hope. Although the phone call was made to my dad, it was the call that redirected my life path and career.

SHIFTING GEARS: DREAMING IS THE BEGINNING OF PLANNING

My father had been accepted into Factory Five Racing's 3-day Automotive Build School, which allows 12 students each month to build a Factory Five Mk4 Roadster, the Shelby Cobra replica car. Led by instructors from Mott Community College in Flint, Michigan, students travel to Factory Five's site in Flint to train in a 3-day seminar. My father was granted reimbursement for his travel expenses and the school's tuition and was donated a Factory Five component kit to build his own Mk4 Roadster. By practicing at the Build School, he learned, sharpened, and tested his skills, in preparation for one day building his own Shelby Cobra.

After the 3-day seminar, he felt like he knew everything there was to know about building a Factory Five car and seemed confident about moving forward with his own project. He relied on the connections he made with other students at the seminar, some of whom lived in northern New Jersey or western Pennsylvania—within driving distance of where we lived. Through this training, he learned tips and insight from those who traveled this path before him. He also joined a club of novices and veterans alike—mostly older, retired male mechanics or engineers—who were involved in multiple builds or had recently completed their build and wanted to show off their finished product.

When he returned from Michigan, he brought with him not only an enhanced enthusiasm for cars, but a newfound enthusiasm for life. He had always been interested in and passionate about cars—like many men in America—but this experience showed him that he could exercise that passion toward positive action. He developed practical experience; he learned the principles and fundamentals of building his own car from professional instructors; and now with his kit in possession, he was revitalized and poised to replicate that experience over the next few years.

I still remember the night we picked up his kit from a loading dock in the Ironbound section of Newark, New Jersey, with miles of junkyards and auto shops around us. It was windy and stormy, which made it a miserable night, but somehow the two of us made the drive fun, discussing how dynamic this endeavor would be and what this meant to our family and community. We secured the kit that night and brought it back to our home and immediately opened it up. We were so excited we didn't even notice the time—it was approaching midnight. It felt like Christmas morning to my father, giddy at the glance of the car's front end, drive shaft, an exterior shell, and all of the critical parts of the car. Now the challenge would be to: (1) accumulate the other pieces; and (2) put the pieces together. This is where my father's lifelong resourcefulness came into play.

We talked about the day when the project would be finished, and how all of our neighbors and friends would celebrate, taking pictures of us and asking for turns to ride in the passenger seat. He talked about build parties, where he would invite his new buildmates to our home to help him build on the weekend, and we would order pizza, chicken wings, breadsticks, and perhaps, when the day was over, refresh ourselves with a cold beer (or two). We talked about how great it would be if we could build this, together, in partnership. I soon started lifting some of the heavy equipment, fastening some of the nuts and bolts, and tightening some of the screws. Every cut and every measurement seemed like a high stakes activity with pending disaster if we were off by even a few millimeters.

Months into our journey, I started to notice the feel of every hand I shook at work, and I laughed to myself as I compared each one to my father's. I'd always marvel at my father's rough, calloused hands which became stronger and stronger—tightly correlated with his raising self-confidence and self-esteem—as he continued to teach himself new ways of accomplishing similar tasks and functions. I started to see him smile more and enjoy life more. With all that he was going through, trying to find work and support himself as well as the guilt of asking me to make an even more significant financial contribution to the upkeep of our household, I realized that he was finally passionate about something. He had a dream and turned that dream into goals. And one day, as if witnessing this outside of his own body, he would turn that dream into a milestone and into something tangible. The car would one day be licensed, insured, and would soon wreak havoc throughout our neighborhood.

As the process progressed, I started thinking about my own dreams and my own passions. I started to ask myself questions about the things that I wanted to see happen for my community and the world, and I situated myself in those dreams. What were some of the things I wanted to happen for me and my father? Was I soulfully fulfilled? If not, what were the activities and events that gave me that fulfillment? I was at a point in my own professional journey that caused me significant anguish, and I was coming home disgusted with myself—for not only contributing to some of the larger social ills that I used to fight against, but more selfishly, forgoing my own dreams for larger financial rewards. Perhaps I wanted what my father had at the time: He had something that stimulated him, mentally and emotionally. Although he didn't have a degree in mechanical engineering or any formal training other than the 3-day seminar in Michigan, and he didn't have all the financial resources in the world to support the purchase or trading of an engine, equipment, parts, or accessories, he still found a way to put his 100,000 piece puzzle together. With meticulous attention to detail, unrelenting vigor, and the resourcefulness of a hustler, he put it together. By showing me a way, he helped me put it together. He paved the road and gave me a map that would provide guidelines toward accomplishing the same thing in my own life. I planned around my passion and would soon turn that passion into my career.

FAMILY, CAREER DEVELOPMENT, AND HIGHER EDUCATION

In retrospect, I finally made meaning of my life by openly reflecting on an intricate grid of intimate personal and communal experiences. Moreover, registering my father's challenges and triumphs helped me put my own aspirations into larger perspective, speaking to my happiness and fulfillment more than money or allure ever could. Certainly, there are few decisions that exert as profound an influence on people's lives as the choice of a field of work or career (Hackett & Betz, 1995). There is growing evidence that the degree to which students in higher education feel supported in this process by their institutions is not simply a function of the assistance level they experience with resume preparation, interview skill building, networking, time management, and effective letter writing. Institutional staff—particularly those at career development centers—must also generate relevant points of contact that will increase the exposure to and responsiveness of the needs of historically marginalized student populations (Herr, Heitzmann, & Rayman, 2006). In my case, observing my father's pursuit was pivotal in my own career development. And if more students were encouraged to further engage and reflect on the professional lessons taught by their own families, it might lead to sound career exploration and build a sense of purpose and agency in students.

During any prevailing social and economic conditions, career development and exploration is the foundation on which a core life path must be based (Rayman, 1993). However, with the significant omission of a space to incorporate the experiences of family—the struggles and challenges as well as the triumphs and accomplishments—the progress toward self-discovery and exploration is often impeded. This does a disservice to those students who come to rely on their families as educational and professional allies. Therefore, colleges and universities need to be cognizant of the interdependent family and communal value systems when implementing academic and professional programs and practices for all students.

Understanding the factors that contribute to professional discovery and pursuit continues to be an area of unknowns for colleges and universities. Although it is important to consider the creation of a positive environment within the college, it is equally valuable to understand the environment outside the college with which students continue to be connected (Maramba & Palmer, 2011). For me, my father was one such factor that played an important part in my life, and more specifically, his support and inspiration influenced my process of self-discovery and played an important role in my college and professional success.

It is my hope that college educators and administrators consider how institutional practices impact students and their relationship with the parents, guardians, and families from which they derive. The development of culturally relevant and socially practical programs, practices, and policies, within the academic and social environment, are critical to facilitating and strengthening student development during the college years. Providing opportunities for students to engage their experience with their families and communities, with hopes to help them activate their personal and professional interests, allows them to be more present in their own academic experience. Through more expansive outreach programs and practices, and creating mechanisms by which students feel empowered by sharing their academic experience with their family, and incorporating their experience with their family on campus, college administrators can help nurture the adjustment for all students, particularly those from communities where a strong connection to family and culture is critical to survival and sustainability. For me, sharpening my reverence for learning from my father literally changed my life. It was my father who helped me to develop a purpose in life, not a career center.

Just like my father, I eventually laid down a strategy to pursue my own dreams. I left my job at the capital markets firm to pursue a graduate degree in college student affairs. This allowed me to learn the professional competencies and develop the skills to, hopefully, provide a platform for students to commit the same type of self-discovery and dream attainment that I experienced. With no doubts and no regrets, I made the sharp transition to work for a non-profit education research organization in Washington, DC, investigating ways to increase access to and success in our nation's post-secondary education system. Although I may not make as much money as I made before, every time I catch myself thinking about what I do or don't have, I always remember that my father reared me and provided me with everything I needed—on a fraction of the compensation I currently receive for my work. I guess unknowingly, that's his way of silently reminding me to be thankful for the things I *do* have.

Although I reside hundreds of miles away from my father, every so often I find myself in a steady gaze that remains fixed on the man who devoted his life to me. I'm content and fortunate that I've been given a foundation on which to live, a reason for which to strive, and the experience of having seen a dream accomplished right before my eyes. Once or twice a year I get to see him, and we take a spin in the Cobra. Occasionally, I ask him if he thinks I would ever accomplish a feat as incredible as his. With a sincere grin, and the wisdom symbolized in the very car in which we sit, he turns to me and remarks, "Son, you accomplished that a long time ago. . . . You accomplished that when you were born. And as long as your passion is your career, every new day unveils an opportunity to bring you closer to new dreams."

REFERENCES

Austin, A. (2009). *Getting good jobs to America's people of color.* Washington, DC: Economic Policy Institute.

Austin, A. (2010). *Uneven pain—Unemployment by metropolitan area and race.* Washington, DC: Economic Policy Institute.

Coles, R., & Green, C. (2009). *Dismissing the myth: The persistence of black fatherhood in America.* New York: Columbia University Press.

Hackett, G., & Betz, N. E. (1995). Career choice and development. In J. E. Maddux (Ed.), *Self-efficacy, adaptation, and adjustment; Theory, research, and application* (pp. 249–280). New York: Plenum.

Hamer, J., & Marchioro, K. (2002). Becoming custodial dads: Exploring parenting among low-income and working-class African-American fathers. *Journal of Marriage and Family, 64*(1), 116–129.

Herr, E. L., Heitzmann, D. E., & Rayman, J. R. (2006). *The professional counselor as administrator: Perspectives on leadership and management of counseling services   across settings.* San Francisco: Routledge.

Lerman, R. I., & Sorensen, E. (2000). Father involvement with their nonmarital children: Patterns, detriments, and effects on their earnings. *Marriage & Family Review, 29*(2), 137–158.

Livingston, G., & Parker, K. (2011). *Tale of two fathers: More are active, but more are absent.* Washington, DC: Pew Research Center.

Maramba, D. C., & Palmer, R. T. (2011). Perceptions of family support among students of color at a predominately white university. *Enrollment Management Journal 5*(3), 110–133.

Pew Research Center. (2010). *How the great recession has changed life in America: A balance sheet at 30 months.* Washington, DC: Pew Research Center.

Pitts, L. (1999). *Becoming dad: Black men and the journey to fatherhood.* Atlanta, GA: Longstreet.

Rayman, J. (1993). Contemporary career services: Theory defines practice. *New Directions for Student Services: The Changing Role of Career Services, 62,* 3–23.

Tsoi-A-Fatt, R. (2010). *We dream a world: The 2025 vision for black men and boys.* Washington, DC: Center for Law and Social Policy.

11 Unconventional Genius
Father Knows Best

Toby S. Jenkins

I went to college as an undergraduate during the years when student records were beginning to evolve technologically. Grade reports were still mailed to the parent's home but the university was just beginning to offer students an opportunity to electronically check their final grades before receiving the official paper grade report. I knew I had done well my first semester so I rushed to the computer almost daily to get updates on my semester grades. When they were all in I made A's in all of my courses—a 4.0 my first semester of college. When my father came home, I rushed out to tell him the good news: "Daddy I got all A's—a 4.0!!" My father looked at me like I was crazy and then he became serious. "Now Toby, I know you are used to making all those A's in high school but this is *college*. You may not get the same grades you got before and that's okay. You know Carolina isn't a place where A's come easy." I tried to tell my dad that I already knew for sure my grade report. But he still responded with an exasperated, "I just don't want you to be disappointed. We're proud of whatever grades you make as long as you stay in school." Then my grade report finally came to the house. I didn't open it. I simply handed it to my father. I will never forget that when my father opened the report, he stood for what seemed like hours just staring at it and shaking his head. He carried it with him everywhere—posted it on the announcement board at work. He kept saying to me, "I can't believe it. You got all A's at the university!" At that moment, I realized that my father's initial skepticism was not about him not believing in me. "College" was a big deal to him because he had never been. To him, "college" was both the ultimate dream and a difficult and mystical world. "College" meant something special. In his mind just getting there and graduating would be a major accomplishment. And so he was overwhelmed when faced with the idea that not only could his daughter go to college but she could conquer it—that she wouldn't just make it through this experience but she would come out on top. And as I progressed through school and continued to excel in many different ways, my father's enthusiasm for the idea of my high performance—his amazement at the audacity of my collegiate success never waned. When I won the award for the highest GPA among all black graduates at my university—my father cried. When I was selected as one of the Top 25 Most Promising Minority Advertising students in the country—my father cheered. I was a little scared that when I finally walked across the stage he might have a heart attack. But I understand why all of this was so amazing to him. He was in awe of the fact that a black janitor and mill worker from South Carolina could create something so outstanding. You see, we are an extension of our parents—I am his seed, his skin, his spirit, his values, beliefs, and dreams. And so my success was not my own—he had something to do with it.

My father was a worker. He worked three jobs for most of my life. And so he was rarely home and when he was at home he was usually asleep. He'd never say that he had bad jobs—my father enjoyed the idea of work, he appreciated it, and he loved the community that is present at a job. So a life of constant work was both a sacrifice and a reward. But even with him being constantly away at a job, somehow he managed to still be a parent—to teach us important lessons through example. I didn't appreciate this until I became an adult and began working professionally. For many years, I spent time working as a student affairs practitioner in higher education, often facilitating leadership development workshops for college students. I would use many different leadership theories, but one theory that was popular many years ago was Kouzes and Posners (2002) "Leadership Challenge." In the leadership challenge, they list five practices of exemplary leaders: (1) model the way; (2) inspire a shared vision; (3) challenge the process; (4) enable others to act; and (5) encourage the heart. I had taught this leadership model for many years, but it wasn't until I stepped into an actual administrative leadership role (not just teaching) that I realized I had first learned these principles from my dad. My father exhibited bits and pieces of each of these practices. When I am with my dad I always feel loved and accepted without condition. He nurtures my heart. Both he and my mother inspired a vision of living life guided by a moral compass and with a commitment to making a contribution. My dad challenged the social limits that were put on both himself and his family. If as a black man with a high school education, he could not get a job paying him a decent salary, he would work three of them to get the salary necessary to take care of his family. He never gave up or gave in. He found a way around things. And as a parent, he never crippled us with his own expectations of us. He allowed us to be free to explore whom we were from softball, to band, cheerleading to student council, banking intern to Oscar Mayer Wienermobile driver, my father was proud of each random thing that I did and gave me the courage to act on all of my passions and interests regardless of how vastly different they all were. This single ethic has helped me to create a pretty incredible life that knows no boundaries. I enjoy my life because my father enabled me to do so.

But more than any other leadership practice, my dad modeled the way. Good leaders are a work of art. They are an exhibition of principal and dedication; they are a portrait of diligence and determination. And so was my dad. Sometimes I'm now the one standing in wonder, shaking my head at the dedication he showed to our family. It is so very easy for a man to pick up and leave his family. The less difficult road is one that allows you to simply walk away unwilling or unable to make the necessary sacrifices to take care of your responsibilities—working multiple and hard jobs; going without personal conveniences to afford things for your children, or simply sticking it out and enduring the struggle that comes with creating a family with modest means. And so the fact that my father not only stayed, but in many ways gave the whole of his life to us—all of his time was spent working for us—that means the world to me. I know for sure that I work so hard and relentlessly because my dad first showed me what it means to be dedicated to something—to give everything you have to your commitments. We need this type of humility and commitment in our companies, organizations, and communities. What are you willing to do out of love and commitment for those that you serve? How hard are you willing to work and what are you willing to sacrifice?

Working in student affairs at a university is definitely a pleasant job. We really don't have much to complain about—many people would love to have our jobs. Our work is meaningful, challenging, fun, and rewarding. But we do work long hours. When I look back on how many hours I worked while in student affairs on any given week, I'm amazed that I had that type of stamina. But even at times when I wanted to complain about being on campus at midnight or working on a Saturday—I remembered my father. How dare I complain—he worked hard so I could work well. As I now sit in pleasant and loving work environments, in beautiful offices on well-manicured campuses, I am always called to remember the back-breaking work that so many others, including my father, endured, so that I could live to sit in a director's chair. And so I sat there late at night or on the weekend and I worked for as long as it took to create a product or outcome that made me proud.

My dad modeled humility. It takes a lot of humility to pick up other people's trash so that your children can live a beautiful life. He turned garbage and steel machines into something beautiful—an act of love. It was he who taught me how to be a good leader—to transform mediocrity into excellence. He also taught me something about spirit and leadership. Most parents have a story that they constantly tell. They tell it so much that you can repeat it word for word. My father loved to tell the story of how he worked as a janitor at the lieutenant governor's mansion in South Carolina. Many of the professionals that worked there would walk by him as if he didn't exist. But the lieutenant governor always stopped to talk and made time to care. He would ask my dad how his daughter was doing at Carolina—he remembered the details of my dad's life. That truly touched my father. And so, he would always say to me, "I know you're going to have a big job some day. When you get your big job, always speak to the janitors. Treat everybody like people, like they matter." I never forgot that.

When I became director of the cultural center at Penn State, I always made time to form relationships with the custodial staff that cleaned my building. I never asked any of my staff to do anything I wasn't willing to do. So I hauled supplies, set up events, and stayed to clean up after programs along with my staff. If I asked anyone to pick up trash or sweep floors after an event, I would be right there beside them cleaning, too. I allowed our work-study students to bring their children to work. It is difficult going to school and being a single parent. We had a library and so we allowed that to be a space where the kids of our student employees could come after school, free of charge, and do homework and be safe until their parents were done with work. And we all loved those kids like a true community should. No book or class taught me how to lead with my heart—my parents did that. I learned to have a big heart because my father gave me his.

My dad also modeled financial responsibility. When I was in college, I was a public relations/advertising major and so I never took any finance courses. But I didn't need any formal instruction because I already had a master teacher showing me the way. We need to resist the notion that leaders, educators, and artisans reside outside of the homestead. My own parents never went to college but they were brilliant examples of how to make ends meet when both ends are ragged and cut short. Before Suze Orman, for me, there was Bennie and Joyce. They never made a high income, but we never wanted for anything. They never had debt—ever. They never lived above their means. So when school trips, instruments, and other opportunities were crucial we could always "afford it." They were brilliant financial advisors. Regardless of his modest income, my dad's financial affairs were so in order and his credit rating so good that he could essentially get anything he wanted—no one ever told him no. There are many people making three times the salary of my dad, that can't even get approved for a small department store credit card. I learned from my parents that money isn't everything but the management of it matters. You can afford a lot with very little if you know how to sacrifice and save. If I hadn't had this model to guide me, the money that going to college allowed me to make would have meant nothing.

My dad always calls me a genius. He continues to be in awe of my mind and my achievements. He truly believes that I am special, not just smart. And I feel the same way about him. My father is a genius and so are many parents like him. I often comment that a doctoral degree is not a measure of intelligence—it is a measure of your ability to endure, to follow direction. Genius is something different. Genius is about innovative, creative, and transformative thinking. Genius is about solving problems that might intimidate others. Geniuses create new things—new inventions, new ways of thinking, and in my father's case, new life histories. In my 2011 article, "A Beautiful Mind: Black Male Intellectual Identity and Hip Hop Culture," I argue for a new way to conceptualize the idea of genius:

More public critiques are needed of the traditional conceptualization of "genius" as being Western, White, and male. . . . In contemporary public blogs, these outdated ideologies still persist. A 2008 blog post sharing the "Top 50 Geniuses of All Time" listed 50 White men from the Western world (http://4mind4life.com/blog/2008/03/30/list-of-geniuses-top-50-influential-minds/). New ways to define and appreciate genius and intellectual contributions must be developed. Clearly, people of color, women, radical activists, and many political prisoners have transformed our society for the better in deep and meaningful ways. They have pushed to expand our laws, our behavior, and our thinking. (Jenkins, 2011 p 1231)

And that's what my dad did. He pushed to expand the possibilities in our family. He pushed to expand my understanding of a work ethic, a moral code, and a life purpose. I am smart. I am a high achiever. I am exceptional. But even more than the reality of whom I have become, what now makes my dad stand in wonder and shake his head is the simple fact that I came from him. In spite of his level of education, income, or social status, he made a college professor. Literally. He often whispers, "You've done all of these things . . . and I made you. I made you." Yes, dad, you did.

REFERENCES

Jenkins, T. (2011). A beautiful mind: Black male intellectual identity in hip hop. *Journal of*
Black Studies. November 2011, vol. 42 no. 8 1231–1251
Kouzes, J., & Posner, B. (2002). *Leadership challenge*. San Francisco: Jossey Bass.

Part IV
Community

12 Third Culture Students
Accounting for Family, Distance, and Separation of American-Born and Internationally-Raised U.S. College Students

Aracelie L. Castro

There are many non-traditional students attending college today. Many contemporary college students are significantly older or have come with large family obligations like being a parent. There are also some who may in fact be the traditional age of 18 but are culturally different because they have lived most or all of their developmental years in a country other than the U.S. This group of students is known as Third Culture Kids, or TCKs (after the age of 18, they are referred to as Adult TCKs, or ATCKs). Many of these students' families are living overseas at the time that they begin preparing for college. TCKs return to the U.S. while their families continue to live overseas. This chapter, which is motivated by my personal experience as a military child, focuses on the existing literature on TCKs, paying particular attention to the emotions experienced by both TCKs and their families during the process of going to college.

THIRD CULTURE KIDS DEFINED

In order to understand the unique challenges TCKs face when applying for and beginning college, one must become familiar with this group. TCK-World, a website designated as the official home of Third Culture Kids, defines a TCK as:

> a person who has spent a significant part or all of his or her develop-mental years outside the original culture of their parents. The third culture kid builds relationships to all the cultures, while not having full ownership of any. Although elements from each culture are assimilated into the third culture kid's life experience, the sense of belonging is in relationship to others of the same background, other TCKs. (www. tckworld.com, 2010)

In other words, the original or *first culture* is that of the parents, the *second culture* is that of the host country, and the shared culture formed in between the two becomes the *third culture* (Pollock & Van Reken, 2009). In keeping with these definitions, the term TCK is often applied to sons and daughters of military personnel, federal civilians, missionary workers, and international businesspeople who are "being raised in a highly mobile" and "genuinely cross-cultural world" (Pollock & Van Reken, 2009, p. 16). On the U.S. Department of State website, there is a page dedicated to TCKs. It states:

> According to Kay Eakin, author of *According to My Passport, I'm Coming Home*, the term TCK was first used 40 years ago by Ruth Hill Useem in her research on North American children living in India. She and subsequent others found that TCK's cope rather than adjust, becoming both "a part of" and "apart from" whatever situation they are in. Mobile kids tend to have more in common with each other than with their American peers who have not had internationally mobile experiences. The family and international peer group has played a large role in their formation setting them apart when they return to the US. (http://www.state.gov/m/dghr/flo/c21995.htm)

Because they often feel cultural distance from American society, TCKs tend to have a stronger need to quickly develop deep friendships and systems of support than other students. Their need to feel secure and adjusted is strong. David C. Pollock and Ruth E. Van Reken's book *Third Culture Kids: Growing Up Among Worlds* takes a comprehensive look at TCKs and is frequently mentioned in the more recent literature written about TCKs. The chapter called "Relational Patterns" describes how there are three reasons (besides it being a cultural habit) to jump into relationships more quickly than others—practice, contentment, and a sense of urgency (2009). Forming relationships is a common practice for TCKs. They have often started so many relationships that it is an easy process for them, and because they have had so many diverse experiences, TCKs feel they usually have a relevant contribution to any given conversation. For example, families of Foreign Service Officers and military service members are often required to move every 2 to 3 years as part of the parents' work duties. For the children, that equates to starting a new school after every move. For military children, it could potentially mean two new schools because when moving overseas there have often been waitlists for housing on or near the installation where the parent works every day. This means that upon arrival, some families may live in temporary housing for a period of months while the children attend their first school. When permanent housing becomes available, the families move again and the children may have to change to yet another school. Although the description may seem frantic, the children do not notice as much as one might think. They become accustomed to such a lifestyle and are able to cope with it because their classmates and peers are often "global nomads" experiencing similar highly mobile lifestyles. They are content with the type of life that they have lived and feel confident that others will take an interest in their perspectives. Finally, having moved so often, they realize there may not be time to waste when developing a new relationship because there is always the potential for the parties involved to part ways quickly (Eakin, 1999; Pollock & Van Reken, 2009). Forming pseudo-familial bonds is an urgent task for TCKs. Pollock and Reken (2009) offer the following example:

> Most expatriate families live far from relatives and tend to reach out to one another as surrogate families in times of need. When there is a coup, it's the friends in this international community who are together in the fear, the packing, the wondering, and the leaving. Without a doubt, a great deal of bonding that lasts a lifetime takes place at such times. (p. 136)

And so, TCKs value their immediate family members and find extended family members in their fellow TCKs and expatriate neighbors. This is a student population that clearly understands the value of creating community and tapping support networks in order to make it through an experience.

FAMILY INFLUENCE ON COLLEGE CHOICE

Family has a strong influence on the college choice for TCKs. TCKs are often applying to colleges while still living in overseas locations. In some instances, the TCKs may not have spent any of their developmental years in the U.S. This was the circumstance for Shondrika Harvey. Her family was living in Kaiserslautern, Germany, when she departed for college in Texas. She had not lived in the U.S. since she was a 1-year-old, and immediately wanted to return back to Germany. "She felt like a foreigner in her own country" (Soldiersmediacenter, 2007). Josh Cajinarobleto is another example. Although he had lived in the U.S. a total of 6 years while growing up, Josh, who was coming to the University of Florida from Japan, shared the following:

> You think about the average student, maybe they're moving in from a different state or city, but for me, I'm coming from the other side of the world. . . . I'm totally alone, I don't know anybody, I don't have that support system nearby. (Lilly, Jan 2009, p. 26)

Many students like Josh and Shondrika made their college choice sight unseen. According to Cottrell and Useem (1994), many such students choose colleges their parents or friends had attended. In other instances, TCKs may have returned every summer to visit extended family members (e.g., a grandmother, grandfather, aunt, or uncle). In the case of TCKs who regularly visit the U.S., they often apply to schools in or near the cities that they regularly visit. Sometimes they apply at the suggestion of their parents, and in other instances they simply follow in the footsteps of a sibling or friend who did the same. In a study of college choice among U.S. TCKs, Thurston-Gonzalez (2009) found the following:

> Family members were the major source of influence regarding college choice for all student participants. In all cases, one or both parents were cited as the primary influence. In addition, cousins, uncles, aunts, and siblings were also mentioned. Six of the participants mentioned friends who influenced some aspect of their college choice process. (p. 136)

Whether it is attending a parent's alma mater or a school near grandparents, we find that family members are pivotal when it comes to the TCK making the decision of what college to attend.

APPLICATION AND ADMISSION PROCESSES—FAMILIES NEEDED

Once the choices regarding where to apply have been made, the actual application and admissions process begins. As with any student, the college application and admissions process can be an exhilarating yet overwhelming experience for TCKs and their families. All TCK prospective students and their families must consider the same factors as prospective students who are already stateside, such as the cost of the institution, the institution's location, its quality of life, the academic resources available, and the opportunities for personal growth. TCKs and their family members must also pay particular attention to the application and admissions process. In the years prior to the Internet becoming so pervasive, a good deal of communication was done via telephone and post. This meant that in addition to the necessary application fees, many families were also paying additional monies for their international telephone calls to U.S. colleges and stamps for international mail to the U.S. Additionally, TCKs were competing with various time zones in order to coordinate phone calls with admissions offices. Those who lived in South Asia might have been making phone calls in the early hours of the morning in order to speak to the admissions representatives at a school on the East Coast that was 13 or 14 hours behind. Campus visits were a luxury that many families could not afford. This would often result in students attending schools they had never physically seen (Soldiersmediacenter, 2007; Eakin, 1999).

In recent years, the advent of the Internet has allowed many colleges and universities to have most of their required admissions processes and documents available online. Although it is much easier to apply for schools than it may have been in years past, the process still has pitfalls. It seems there is more information available than is palatable. There are now so many options and such a mass of information overload that distinguishing schools from one another has the potential to become a logistical nightmare. The extensiveness of college websites now make the campus visit even more necessary to filter the information and to get a true feel for the school. The other pitfall of the Internet is that not all TCKs have easy access to it. Some TCKs and their families may be posted in remote areas of the world without quality or sometimes any Internet access. In these situations, the TCKs will rely more heavily on their families and communities to ensure all that needs to be accomplished for their college application and entrance is completed in a timely fashion. Again, family is a critical part of the process.

MY TCK MEMORY

I would like to share the story that inspired me to do this chapter. Although I was living in the U.S. when it was my time to apply to colleges and universities, I witnessed much of what is described in the literature when my oldest brother was in high school. We lived in the Republic of Panama in the years before the Internet and moved back to the U.S. the summer after he graduated from high school. I recall that during his junior year, my mother began suggesting schools for him to consider and had him register for the Scholastic Aptitude Test (SAT) and American College Test (ACT). Although I was younger, I remember him filling out several forms and letting me fill in all the bubbles of the accompanying ScanTrons. He would then go to the library to make copies of all the forms, and put them into their respective envelopes to mail back to the U.S. I also remember him checking the mail constantly for his test confirmation information, and later, his test scores.

During the same time period, my mother also suggested he apply to several schools including Our Lady of the Lake College in San Antonio. At that time, it was a small, private, Catholic school in the city where my parents owned a home, and the school my mother had always wanted to attend. Unlike the literature mentioned in this chapter, my brother was adamant about NOT going to that school. However, his first choice for school was the University of Texas at Austin (UT), which was still less than 60 miles from San Antonio, and still relatively close to "home." He was accepted to UT and attended for the first year. He took a break for a few years before going back to a local community college. A few years later, he obtained his degree from the University of Texas at San Antonio (UTSA). Not completing one's degree at the original school of choice and taking time off is a common occurrence among TCKs (Cottrell & Useem, 1994). Much of the existing literature on TCKs focuses on defining this population, understanding how they relate to others, and acknowledging how their backgrounds affect their journey to college. More research is needed on the TCK student's tendency to take time off from college once started or to transfer at some point during their college experience. Persistence and attrition of TCKs should be a major focus of future research.

In addition, very little is mentioned about the emotions experienced by TCKs or their family once the TCK is accepted and goes off to college leaving their family overseas. I cannot speak directly about such a situation because my family and I moved back to San Antonio 2 months after my brother's high school graduation. However, I can share that when we thought we would have to stay another year in Panama, I remember feeling more than a little disturbed. I wondered how life would be without my brother nearby and really only accessible by letters and the occasional phone call. We were never joined at the hip, per se, but I certainly did not like the idea of him leaving us all behind and being so far away. I did not feel I was ready for that. I could only imagine how my parents felt with the possibility of having to let their first born go away to a school they had never even seen and might not be able to visit until his second year. The Department of State has a handbook on its website that briefly addresses the topic (Eakin, 1999). However, there is definitely a need for colleges and universities to make available to the families of TCKs additional resources and forms of support that directly address issues of family separation.

Future research could include personal interviews with TCKs and their families to understand and document their personal experiences. Research might also include a document review or analysis of the many blogs or videos contained on sites such as TCKWorld, YouTube, and Expatriate Exchange in order to discover threads of discussion related to emotions and the personal experiences of these students. An online magazine for TCKs, *Denizen*, dedicates an entire section to the subject of TCKs going to college. It contains articles contributed by TCKs who want to share their college experiences and advice with others (Yiu, 2011). One author wrote a two-part piece where she shared stories of her fellow TCKs at the University of Florida (Lilly, Jan 2009). At UF, one student, Andy L'Esperance, participated in orientation and probably stunned a few people in the room when they asked who had traveled furthest to be there. He had come from Heidelberg, Germany. With this anecdote, the article highlights why, like many TCKs, Andy "found himself gravitating towards people who found travel to be exciting, not scary and impossible" (Lilly, Jan 2009, p. 51). Travel has often been the cornerstone of these students' life experiences. They have initially traveled outside of the U.S. but have probably also traveled throughout their assigned country with their families in order to take advantage of the opportunity to see other parts of the world. And so it makes sense that U.S.-born TCKs might relate more with international students than American students.

In the same article, Lilly (Jan 2009) described her confusion after arriving at the University of Florida, having spent the previous 4 years living in Shanghai:

I didn't have a cell phone that worked in the country. I was jetlagged. The name tag on my dorm door announced that I was from Punta Gorda—a total lie; I had used my grandparents' address as an attempt to get in-state tuition. I saw that another girl was from St. Petersburg, and then realized that she didn't grow up in Russia, rather, a city in Florida. I also discovered that there are cities named Melbourne and Naples, neither of which is in Australia or Italy. (p. 24)

On these online forums, TCKs are writing or commenting on how their lives have been special, enhanced, difficult, or challenging due to their unique experiences. From reading these blogs, important insights can be gained by university administrators, faculty, and TCKs.

HELPING TCKS AND THEIR FAMILIES SUCCEED

What can a college or university do to help TCKs and their families succeed once they decide on a college destination? Wendy Stultz's (2003) article, "Global and Domestic Nomads or Third Culture Kids: Who Are They and What the University Needs to Know," addresses the issue of TCKs adjusting on campus. Some of the suggestions Stultz lists include:

- Allow for appropriate exceptions to rules to be made (i.e., required courses or housing accommodations);
- Determine a way of tracking the retention and graduation rates of this population;
- Encourage TCKs to participate in programming and student organizations;
- Create a method for identifying potential global nomads before matriculation; and
- Determine the priority of TCK support program implementation at a university level, and take actions accordingly. (p. 5)

In the above recommendations, a university can provide invaluable services for TCKs. But as mentioned before, these recommendations still fail to include details regarding family members. The university must become concerned with how to serve the whole of the student—this includes providing space or innovative opportunities for overseas families to also participate in the college experience. During a class discussion at George Mason University, Douglas Little, Director of Orientation and Family Programs and Services at Mason, mentioned how it is more of a trend now for universities to market themselves to the parents of prospective students just as much, if not more than, they market to the students (Little, 2010). This method of recruiting could prove to be priceless in the world of TCKs, where, as discussed earlier, the family greatly influences the student's college choice.

One method for doing so is to create a specific directory and possibly a webpage for TCK families to contact one another. This can serve as an effort to bring them closer to the university community. As discussed earlier, support groups are important in the lives of global natives. Both the families and the students are used to connecting with people who share a similar experience. Universities can follow such a model and offer TCK family members a support group prior to the student even arriving on campus. Catering directly to the families' sense of comfort early in the college decision-making process makes the families feel part of the experiences and thus, could be an effective tool in retaining and graduating TCKs.

Orientations are also vital to TCKs and their families because it is often the first time the TCK is encountering the school. "Higher Education's 'Hidden Immigrants,'" in the National On-Campus Report gives two reasons to have TCK-specific orientations (2005). The first reason is to let TCKs know they have a peer group of others like them on campus. One suggestion for doing this is to involve other students. As stated before, TCKs value their friendships and they "display a high level of continuing international activity such as speaking foreign languages, traveling abroad, and engaging in internationally related occupational and/or volunteer activities" (Cottrell, 1993, p. 2). In this respect, internationally-focused student organizations can be invited to welcome the new TCKs and offer an opportunity for making new friends. Often these are the individuals who will eventually become "surrogate" family members of the new TCKs. By tailoring actions during orientations, schools are able to make it a pleasurable experience for the TCK while easing the minds of family members.

The second reason for offering TCK-specific orientations is to make faculty aware that such a group exists (Higher Education's, 2005). In addition to inviting faculty members to attend potential breakout sessions or panel discussions, schools might also consider incorporating TCK information sessions or panel discussions into faculty orientations. Self-identified TCK students and/or TCK faculty members might lead the discussions and increase non-TCK faculty awareness. The sessions could be recorded and/or streamed live for individuals at other locations or for future viewing and reference by faculty who are unable to attend. Finally, faculty who are aware of TCKs may consider asking TCK students to conduct presentations or panels for courses or seminars. In this way, the TCKs are appreciated for their life experiences and other members of the institution are able to capitalize on those experiences. The community gains knowledge and moves not only toward becoming more globally competent, but also toward creating better global citizens.

TCKs and their families are a special group of individuals who face additional challenges when it is time to prepare a student to enter college or university in the U.S. By being aware that this group exists, by taking more opportunities to understand the complex impact of family and community on this population, and by developing services that address these issues, higher education institutions can literally help to make the ocean divide between students and their families, between home and college, and between fear and success, seem small.

REFERENCES

Cottrell, A. B. (1993, November). *ATCKs have problems relating to their own ethnic groups*. Retrieved April 23, 2010, from www.tckworld.com/useem/art4/html

Cottrell, A. B., & Useem, R. H. (1994, March). *ATCKs maintain global dimensions throughout their lives*. Retrieved April 22, 2010, from www.tckworld.com/useem/art5.html

Eakin, K. B. (1999). Coming "home" to college. In *According to my passport, I'm coming home*, 9. Retrieved January 28, 2012, from http://www.state.gov/documents/organization/2065.pdf

Higher Education's "Hidden Immigrants." (2005, April 1). *National On-Campus Report, 33*, 5–6.

Lilly, C. (2009, January). Part 1: TCK goes to college. *Denizen*. Retrieved January 28, 2012, from www.denizenmag.com

Lilly, C. (2009, August). Part 2: Un-masking me. *Denizen*. Retrieved January 28, 2012, from www.denizenmag.com

Little, D. (2010, April 26). Class discussion with Douglas Little, Director of Orientation and Family Programs and Services. Fairfax, VA.

Pollock, D. C., & Van Reken, R. E. (2009). *Third Culture Kids: Growing up among worlds*. Boston, MA: Nicholas Brealey Publishing.

Soldiersmediacenter. (Producer). (2007). *3rd culture kid*. [Web video]. Retrieved April 23, 2010, from http://www.youtube.com

Stultz, W. (2003). *Global and domestic nomads or Third Culture Kids: Who are they and what the university needs to know* [Web article]. Retrieved April 22, 2010, from www.colostate.edu

TCKWorld: The official home of Third Culture Kids. [Web page]. Retrieved April 22, 2010, from www.tckworld.com

Third Culture Kids. [Web page]. Retrieved April 22, 2010, from www.state.gov

Thurston-Gonzalez, S. J. (2009). *A qualitative investigation of the college choice experiences and reentry expectations of U.S. American Third Culture Kids* (Doctoral dissertation). Loyola University: Chicago. Retrieved April 23, 2010, from ProQuest Digital Dissertations (AAT 3367137).

Yiu, S. (2011, September). A Third Culture Kid's guide to college. *Denizen*. Retrieved January 28, 2012, from www.denizenmag.com

13 *Feminist Ujamaa*
Transnational Feminist Pedagogies, Community, and Family in East Africa

Marla L. Jaksch

INTRODUCTION

As a first-generation college graduate, my life has been transformed through both an engagement and critical reading of education, especially in relation to feminism and feminist pedagogies. It was through my discovery of feminist theory that I began to understand my love–hate relationship with education in a much more complicated way. Feminist theories of education allowed me to see the ways in which I was imagined (or not), excluded, tracked, socialized, and positioned as a working class girl of multiple ethnicities. I was able to clearly understand that educational institutions compartmentalized me in this way through simultaneous racialized, classed, and gendered discourses and practices (Walkerdine, 1998; Lather, 1991; hooks, 1994; Middleton, 1993; Luke and Gore, 1992). It was within educational spaces that I became aware of and ashamed of my class upbringing and where I learned what it is to be a "good girl," in rather limited, painful, and sexist ways (Jaksch, 2003).

But feminist educational spaces have also opened up for me spaces of belonging and freedom. It is through my feminist education that I have come to understand the ways education might also be a tool to rethink and end oppressive and unequal power relations (Freire, 1970; hooks, 1994). Critical and feminist approaches to teaching compel us to "confront the biases that have shaped teaching practices in our society and to create new ways of knowing, different strategies for the sharing of knowledge" (hooks, 1994, p. 12). Feminist cultural critic bell hooks (1994, 2003) has written extensively on the role of community as a necessary component of educational transformation. hooks does not view education or pedagogy as primarily an individual experience, rather she recasts education as a community project—linking education to communities of learners beyond the walls of schools, colleges, and universities to homes, families, communities. Although strategies for cultivating community have been a concern to all social justice-based movements, the work of Black feminists in challenging myths about prevailing dominant notions of community has been tremendous. Patricia Hill Collins (1990) argues that Black women's experience and action in struggle (civil rights, Black power, and women's liberation movements) provides a vision of community that stands in opposition to dominant (white supremacist, patriarchal) culture. According to Collins, the vision of community sustained by women of color as bloodmothers, community mothers, churchmothers, and othermothers serves to challenge social norms that are based on classist, heteronormative, sexist, and Eurocentric social myths. Collins work not only reveals hegemonic norms—she reveals the ways in which we can exert power and become empowered *through* community. Prevailing views of community are commonly presented as arbitrary, competitive, and maintained through relations of dominance. Collins asks us to look at the particular ways women of color envision and create community through connections, caring, and personal accountability as an alternative model for feminist collaboration and activism.

According to hooks (1994), one of the ways that we transgress boundaries, transform power relations, and create community is through dialogue. For many feminist pedagogues, creating a community of learners, in which learners are able to find their own voices in relation to others and address these highly personal and emotionally charged issues together, has been a central prerequisite to doing social justice work (hooks, 1994; Shrewsbury, 1987). Barbara Smith has argued that "making coalitions with people that are different from you " (quoted in Collins, 1990, pp 223) is radical and important. One of the challenges to this has been discovering models for dialogue and community building—especially in light of how essential creating critical communities is as the basis for creating and sustaining change. International, global, and transnational feminists have all discussed the problems of assuming a shared connection based on gender or gender oppression—whether it be as a result of patriarchy, capitalism, globalization, culture, imperialism, or essentialized notions of "woman" or "women." In fact some feminists (mostly from the West) have often uncritically assumed connections with other women on the basis of a global "sisterhood," or in other familial terms (Robin Morgan, 1996; 2003). Although this terminology and the assumptions that undergird this language have been roundly critiqued (Oyerunke Oyewumi, 2003) over the years feminists have not completely abandoned the idea, rather they continue to search for more critical ways to form links with one another (Grewal & Kaplan, 1994; Mohanty, 2003; Ferree & Tripp, 2006; Naples & Desai, 2002).

IF NOT A GLOBAL SISTERHOOD?: TRANSNATIONAL FEMINIST THEORIES AND PEDAGOGIES OF COMMUNITY AND ACTIVISM

As a result of opportunities to study, research, and work within feminist communities outside of the U.S., I have been deeply moved and challenged by transnational feminist theories and activism. A part of my work as a teacher-scholar-activist has been to transnationalize my own teaching and research. I began to seek out ways to bridge my work in the community and in the classroom together, and this community engaged scholarship led me beyond the communities I knew and beyond the locations I had experienced. To transnationalize my teaching has meant not only increasing students' global awareness and building intercultural understanding and communication, but to do so using models that challenge dominant Western paradigms. This is important for several reasons. First, when we transnationalize our teaching it demands that we engage with the impacts and discourses of colonialism, globalization, and neo-liberal forms of capitalism. To do so encourages situating our work within a much larger context and therefore challenging the dominance of academic knowledge focused so heavily on a U.S.-only context or from a U.S.-dominated or Eurocentric perspective. In this way, transnational approaches focus on the interconnectivity of people—between and among individuals and other entities regardless of nation-state. Not in some simplistic, utopian way, but hopefully, in a more complicated, nuanced way. But how this happens becomes a challenging question.

In a now famous 1988 essay, "Can the Subaltern Speak?" (Nelson & Grossberg, 1988) Gayatri Spivak expresses her concern for the processes whereby post-colonial studies re-inscribe, co-opt, and repeat neo-colonial imperatives of political domination, economic exploitation, and cultural erasure. In other words, is the post-colonial critic unknowingly complicit in doing the work of imperialism? She argues that post-colonialism is specifically first-world, male, privileged, academic, institutionalized discourse that surveys and classifies the East (and South) in the same ways that colonialism modes do—by attempting to dismantle it. Her larger argument was that although the attempt to re-appropriate Gramsci's term "subaltern" (the economically dispossessed) to be used as a tool to locate and re-establish a "voice" or collective agency will necessarily be highly problematic. The problem lies in the fact that this is often approached from the outside in order to ameliorate the condition of the oppressed by granting them collective speech rather than letting them speak for themselves. Spivak suggests that this will create the following problems: (1) speaking collectively will result in the assumption of cultural solidarity among heterogeneous people, and (2) it will establish dependence upon Western intellectuals to "speak for" the subaltern condition rather than allowing them to speak for themselves. By speaking out and reclaiming a collective cultural identity, Spivak argues, subalterns will re-inscribe their subordinate position in society. In this way the assumption of subaltern collectivity becomes akin to an ethnocentric, essentialist myth.

Transnational feminist work has focused on how we might work together across differences and borders and look at the ways in which Western feminism has also been implicated in imperialist projects. This is not the "global sisterhood" advocated by Robin Morgan (1984), but rather, draws on the work of women of color feminists such as Patricia Hill Collins (1990) and

Gloria Anzaldua (1984) who see transnational feminist spaces as spaces of conflict, contradiction, and contact in which women, women of color, and other marginalized groups have transformed discourses and spaces that exclude them into spaces of possibility and collaboration. Maylei Blackwell (2005) explains:

> those transformations haven't excluded the notion that those spaces still exclude them or erase them, that there aren't limitations there. I think some the lessons that we take from Gloria Anzaldua is that we transform notions like borders, like spaces of translation and feminist contact, but they're still fraught with violence as well as possibility. (http://www.sscnet.ucla.edu/history/dubois/Transnational%20Feminism.html#_ftn2)

Chandra Mohanty (2003) offers a solidarity model of transnational feminism as the expression of a pedagogy that insists on the centrality of the experiences and strategies of communities of women around the world. Her model allows students to see the "complexities, singularities, and interconnections between communities of women such that power, privilege, agency, and dissent can be made visible and engaged with" (p. 523). Mohanty (2003) argues that differences between people are never just "differences"; "in knowing differences and particulars we can better see connections and commonalities because no border or boundary is ever complete or rigidly determining" (p. 505). The objective is to understand how "specifying difference allows us to theorize universal concerns more fully" (Mohanty, 2003, p. 505). Although not without its problems and criticisms, Mohanty's model centers on the fugitive nature of borders, cultures, and visuality.

Study Abroad and Transnational Feminisms

With concurrent calls for colleges and universities to internationalize and produce more civically engaged students, the proliferation of a range of study abroad programs is not surprising. There has also been an uptick in the development of international service learning programs, which is typically understood as academic instruction with community-based service in an international context. The goals for linking international travel, education, and community include increasing participants' global awareness and development of humane values, building intercultural understanding and communication, and enhancing civic mindedness and leadership skills (Berry & Chisholm, 1999; Hartman & Roberts, 2000).

My goal to transnationalize my teaching has extended to include creating opportunities for students who typically do not have an opportunity to study abroad during college due to socioeconomic and other constraints to study abroad in some manner. Many of my students tell me that they do not see themselves reflected in the location's discourses, images, or as the audience for traditional study abroad programs. Many of my students perceive traditional study abroad as for mostly elite, wealthy, White students. Further, several of my students imagined study abroad as an extended, expensive vacation (which sometimes truly is the case), for which they could not justify taking out high-interest loans or borrowing money to do. Many of my students are unable to afford full-semester long programs, nor are they able to leave the U.S. for extended periods of time due work and/or family responsibilities. *Must opportunities to see and understand the world through travel, study, and exchange remain the domain of wealthy (White) elites?* If the research is to be believed, that students who study abroad have a greater capacity for understanding their own culture through the exploration of another culture, how might priorities be shifted, programs be better defined and implemented, and more locations be developed? And how might we increase the impact of study abroad programs so that participants are learning and creating community in their travel locations?

One way I've begun to challenge current unequal study abroad practices is to understand the history of and the dominant premises for study abroad programs. According to a recent poll by the Institute of International Education, studying abroad has increased by more than 8.5%, becoming a popular rite of passage for many college students. This happens within a global context in which international student migration—the large numbers of international students who cross borders for the pursuit of higher education—in recent years has been addressed and described by many scholars and non-governmental organizations. According to UNESCO (2009),

> In 2007, over 2.8 million students were enrolled in educational institutions outside of their country of origin. This represents 123,400 more students than in 2006, an increase of 4.6%. And the global number of mobile students has grown by 53% since 1999 (with an average annual increase of 5.5%) and by 2.5 times since 1975 with an average annual increase of 11.7% throughout this period. (p. 36)

Many more students than any other time previously are traveling abroad to study. Although the largest follows of students are coming to the U.S. (from China) for undergraduate and terminal degrees, U.S. study abroad happens within the much larger context of international student migration. It is often argued that students will live and work in an increasingly multicultural society and these statistics confirm this.

Unfortunately, as mentioned above, the model that is most dominant in study abroad circles is grounded in neo-liberal discourses concerning the types of *things students will "get"* out of their experiences studying abroad, including, inquiring competitive skills and accumulating cultural capital, and the ability to add a great line highlighting their global travel on their resume for jobs or graduate school. Some program materials problematically suggest that students will become "global citizens" through their travels with little attention to how this process takes place and what is meant by this term exactly.

There has also been a proliferation of service-based study abroad programs that seek to address a presumed gap between theory and practice, with more of a focus on the application of knowledge in a community to address certain needs. Critiques of this model include problems that arise when communities are not a part of the process of deciding whether visitors will be in their communities (sometimes homes and other community spaces) or in what way. For example, this model fails to consider challenges like the need to address when students engage in labor that could be given to a community member who would be compensated for the work, or when students' residential stays make a deep negative impact on community relations.

More recently (at least since 1990), alternative and feminist models of study abroad have been developed. Although some these programs are traditional in that they focus on studying feminism in a global context, in a traditional academic setting, others take place in communities, with organizations or with a combination of these. Some of the critiques of these programs are they may reinforce missionary or Good Samaritan attitudes toward the communities or societies in which they study. Some programs inadvertently reinforce Eurocentrism if students are not provided with the necessary academic work, lack engagement in critical reflection, or if the program is not fully integrated into the community. Although it is extremely helpful for students to cross international borders in order to gain new perspectives and insights, experiential educators Dewey (1938/1997) and Kolb (1984) remind us that international experiences are not in and of themselves educational. As Dewey points out, experiences can be "miseducative" when they have "the effect of arresting or disorienting the growth of further experience" (Dewey, 1938/1997, pp. 131). Experience without critical analysis and reflection is not experiential education; it is simply experience, and the experience may reinforce stereotypes and imperialist ideas unless analyzed and tied to broader bodies of knowledge. Emphasis on analysis builds upon Paulo Freire's (2000) concept of "problem-posing education," which he sees not as "problem-solving" but rather "critical analysis of a problematic reality" (p. 168).

Critical approaches to studying abroad and options for social justice-based programs must be developed and mainstreamed if we are to challenge continued educational inequities and if programs such as these are to be relevant to the majority of our students. In fact, despite some evidence that these types of short-term programs can be successful at meeting many of the objectives mentioned previously, Robbin Crabtree (2008) notes some of the negative outcomes she observed:

- Local children become enamored with foreign students and the material possessions they take for granted;
- Students and other visitors leave piles of used clothing and other "gifts" after the project/trip completion;

- Community members fight about project ownership as development activities exacerbate internal political and interpersonal divisions;
- Members of neighboring communities wonder why no one has come to "help" them;
- Projects reinforce for communities that development requires external benefactors; national governments rely on NGOs to respond to the needs or their country; and
- Many students return to pursue courses of study and careers with little apparent divergence from the path of/toward privilege.

Although these are snapshots Crabtree and others working in the field have shared, it is something I myself have encountered. Challenging these barriers and perceptions has led me to develop a more theoretically grounded, feminist-centered summer program to Tanzania that is neither a traditional service-learning or study abroad program; rather, the model I developed attempts to create an experiential program that puts the problems of transnational collaborating with the communities of women and girls in Tanzania to which we are invited. I have led this evolving program for more than 7 years with more than four different institutions.

Through my work, I've attempted to understand how experiential learning and grassroots development practices serve a critical tools of social transformation, understanding, and change. The benefits of programs like these are many—most of my students initially imagine that they may be traveling far from home to "help" women and girls with their "problems," but they quickly learn that their "problems" are similar, or perhaps, that they may not have the skills, knowledge, or understanding necessary to make change or give advice. Or further still, my students are shocked when they receive and learn as much, if not more, from the women and girls they traveled so far to work with. Opportunities such as these have changed the lives of so many. More than 100 young women (and some young men) have participated in this program (from the U.S.—many more in Tanzania); countless have gone on to work with international women's organizations, decided to study global women's issues or law in graduate school, and several have joined the Peace Corps or served as Fulbright scholars as a result of their international experiences.

Often this type of work counts for little in the tenure process. But as a feminist scholar my career ambitions extend beyond tenure and go deeper than publications. It is my hope to be a part of creating substantial change, especially for those who lack opportunities, through the establishment, continuation, and support of programs and projects that seek to create equity and critical cultural awareness, and fully value the contributions of young girls and women to the world. Barker and Smith (1996) have argued that there is a need for citizens that not only appreciate other cultures, but who understand the differences created by ethnicity and religion and the forces of power and history at work within nations and in international relations.

Critics of short-term, faculty-led trips charge some trips are too brief for students to become fully immersed in another culture and often amount to little more than "academic tourism." Gayatri Spivak (1988) provides a description of the "Third World" becoming a "signifier that allows us to forget that 'worlding.'" Some critics are skeptical of short-term trips suggesting that the length of programs relate to lack of depth and encourage travel that functions similarly to Marx's idea of the "commodity fetish" in which commodity products become part of the process of hiding the network of signs that obscure the history of labor that went into their production. Spivak suggests that the Third World, like the commodity fetish, becomes a sign that obscures its mode of production, thus making Western dominance appear somehow given or natural.

However, I think it is important to note that although I do agree that we must be vigilant in establishing programs that do not encourage the commoditization or fetishization of the global South, its countries, and its communities/culture/art and peoples, we must also be critical of critiques of short programs that necessarily assume a lack of depth and criticality. The types of programs that I have developed and advocate for highlight their need and potential significance if done in thoughtful ways. In fact, although I do not agree with these critiques per se, they have been useful in understanding how, at times, well-intentioned academics reinforce the very thing they wish to dismantle—by insisting that only certain lengths of travel are valid and transformative. By insisting that shorter programs amount to little more than "academic tourism" disregards questions of affordability, privileging wealth (or relative wealth) over the teacher-scholar-activist's role in creating meaningful and thoughtful experiences in the short-term.

Due to this experience—deeply reflecting upon and actively creating transnational study abroad programs in East Africa, combined with my commitment to a transnational feminist pedagogy—I imagined I was prepared to live in and teach at a large Tanzanian university, in a country where I had more than 5 years of travel and research history. In the remainder of this article, I critically reflect on my experiences in Tanzania, teaching in the development studies institute to Tanzanian university students—along with the challenges I faced in applying feminist pedagogical strategies and research methods in the classroom, in building feminist community (in and outside the classroom), and ways in which these struggles had me rethink the *trans* and *national* aspects of my transnational feminist pedagogy and activism.

MY FULBRIGHT YEAR: BUILDING COMMUNITY? THE "OTHER" IN THE OFFICE AND IN THE CLASSROOM

As a scholar equally committed to teaching I applied to the Fulbright Scholars program to Tanzania, which would require undertaking both research and teaching. In preparing my application I read stories of past Fulbright

Scholars—their challenges, the joys, the advice. A pattern emerged from theses stories; teaching and research-based fellowships were incredibly rewarding and notoriously difficult to manage. Much research has gone into supporting the idea of study abroad for students, but does the same hold true for faculty? Up until this time I have devoted most of my time arguing for the necessity of transnationalizing the curriculum for students; now I will shift to a focus on why it may be a necessity for faculty members, too.

According to McCallon and Holmes (2010), "teaching in a study abroad program develops your ability to be innovative and creative, " (http://www.facultyled.com/faculty-led-360-excerpt5/) because when you are at your home campus you have not only your classroom, but the "entire city, culture, people, and more." McCallon and Holmes argue that in this context the process of self-discovery is not just for our students, and that we benefit from the collective experience and interpretation—not just our own. But how might this be different when we are teaching students that are not from the U.S.?

In 2009 I was accepted as a Fulbright Scholar at the University of Dar es Salaam (UDSM) in the Institute of Development Studies. I applied to this program because there were many feminists in the institute and UDSM has a significant historical reputation located in Dar es Salaam, which hosts a significant number of non-governmental organizations (NGOs), community-based organizations (CBOs), civil society organizations, and grassroots organizations—many of them feminist. Since 1970, UDSM has served as a flagship institution in East Africa—the oldest and biggest in Tanzania. Several African presidents are alumni, including current Tanzanian president Jakaya Kikwete and Ugandan president Yoweri Museveni. It has also been the hotbed of pan-African, progressive, and opposition activity, including hosting the likes of Angela Davis, Patricia McFadden, and Walter Rodney.

Challenges in the Classroom: Ethics, Power, and Truth

It is one thing to be a transnational theorist and another to be a transnational teacher! While teaching a graduate level research methods course I learned that students were almost strictly taught quantitative methods; qualitative methods were still viewed as highly suspect. My identity (mzungu, American) and my teaching style (more informal, conversational, and discussion based and feminist!), in combination with the introduction of qualitative research methods that challenged the mainstream approaches they were learning in other classes, caused much consternation among my graduate students. In one class session in particular, where I was teaching participatory action research (PAR) methods, several of my students asked critical questions about the value and ethics in this type of research and how it is achieved. I was co-facilitating this session with a U.S. Ph.D. candidate (M. Maureen Biermann) as she was in Tanzania on a research project piloting a particular PAR method. After reading my students research proposals I felt this approach to development related research might be very useful to many of my students. PAR can reflect an ethical commitment to creating conditions for social change to be used by the community for their own purposes. Kurt Lewin (1948) first mentioned PAR as bridging theory and practice, incorporating planning, action, and investigating the results of actions. PAR originates from two research approaches, namely action research and participatory research. Khanlou and Peter (2005) are of the opinion that PAR is not a method of research, but rather an orientation to research. Therefore, PAR might be further defined as social investigation, educational work, and action.

I imagined students would find this approach useful and a welcome change of approach from the purely quantitative methods they had been introduced to previously. My co-facilitator and I decided to ask the graduate students about barriers to their education at UDSM as the foundation of the PAR exercise. My thinking was that I wanted to find a topic that would engage all students in the process and as a result we could present our informal findings to the graduate program so that they might use it to improve or strengthen their program. The exercise worked well in that students were deeply engrossed in the process, but it also revealed the level of inequality that exists and the implications for their education should they participate in this in-class assignment. What was to follow were several days of heated discussion about truth, ethics, social change, and the impacts of globalization and neo-liberal economic policies on research, jobs, and life in general. I had significantly misunderstood the risks involved in asking students to make visible the institutional constraints to their success. Despite a strong constitution and quota systems that support equity among peoples, too often women, youth, and the poor are caught up in a network of inequalities. Educational institutions, especially UDSM, are part of structural and systemic inequalities even if it is simultaneously a part of challenging them, too. It made me realize how cavalier I had been in teaching these methods and it made me come to terms with the degree to which knowledge is power. For my students to learn these methods and then be expected to generate new findings that may reveal and name the source of new or continued inequality may lead to their dismissal from school, potential jobs, or put their lives at risk. For many of my female students it meant addressing the lack of support for students with children; the frequent sexual harassment they faced on campus, on the streets, in their work, and at home; and the lack of respect for women's knowledge systems.

Communities of Power: Nguvu kwa Jamii

Due to the work that I was doing as a Fulbright Scholar, I was privileged to have access to the U.S. Embassy, receive invites to events at the embassy and the ambassadors residence, and establish contacts at these locations and events. And because the expatriate community in Dar es Salaam is so small, I was able to meet with ambassadors of other countries and their staffs, heads of major NGOs and aid organizations, and Tanzanian government staffers. One of the most common pastimes for expatriates is to discuss how difficult it is to live in Tanzania—how dangerous, the traffic gridlock, and the security. It was easy to get caught up in this activity and at some point I realized that I would much rather be lonely than engage in more of this waste of time. Instead I began to use those times when I was obligated to meet with people in power of an organization, committee, business, or company as an opportunity to ask them to visit my class, mentor a student, or allow a visit from my class to their offices. This eventually led to weekly meetings with students at my home on campus. It was through this, leading informal workshops at my home, that I learned more about my students, their desires, and struggles, and where we began to build community and a home away from home.

We began to meet at my home because it was close to campus, space on campus is difficult to reserve, and many of my students just felt more comfortable meeting informally where they could bring their children or be more relaxed. The norm for faculty–student interaction on campus can be very patriarchal, formal, and hierarchal. We typically shared a meal or snacks with fresh juice (made by my husband no less) while we covered different material. Sometimes it was strictly academic—trying to understand a method, theory, or concept. Other times we watched films, mostly documentary films that a colleague shared with me (Thanks Brian Jara!), that were mostly about African women such as Wangari Maathai, Ellen Sirleaf Johnson or about women's experiences in Liberia, Ethiopia, the Congo, and Egypt. We discussed our lives, how we got to where we were, what we imagined for the future. We told lots of stories! Stories are important because they show us how we make meaning of who we are and what is expected of us, especially as women. This is the everyday material that the majority of scholars have ignored, having deemed it as unimportant.

These meetings certainly had an impact on how the students viewed me as an educator, and in turn, how they imagined themselves in relation to education. I learned so much about my students and developed a few close relationships. Although I first doubted my ability to be an effective mentor to my students, I soon realized that my Tanzanian students where in many ways no different that my U.S.-based students. Much of Western feminist scholarship views Third World or women in Africa in certain ways, often as relatively undifferentiated, united in poverty, and perhaps with a single goal in life. In contrast, our conversations revealed the complicated ways in which women "negotiate against marginalization of their knowledge" (Swai, 2009, p. 5). According to Swai (2009), much of education for women/girls in Africa since colonial times has been concentrated on "women's reproduction, child-care, and childrearing" (p. 6) with the pre-planned agenda of shaping knowledge and skills toward caring for children and becoming good wives, mothers, and helpers, a system which she argues is still very much in place today. Swai argues that education as an institution has been one of the biggest cultural tools used in dislocating women and suppressing their creativity and agency in Africa. In many ways our meetings allowed for my students to critically explore and validate their experiences and chart a new course. Many of my students came from modest backgrounds and they worried about their futures, desired more choices, and also longed for a place in their world. Many of our meetings did not necessarily make them feel more secure, in fact, much of what we shared only complicated their desires. But what we all seemed to get out of the meetings was a connection to each other, a place to go, someone to talk to about it.

But this learning was both personal *and* scholarly. It is my belief that building community opens the door for deep intellectual engagement. It was through these meetings that we were able to make androcentricism, in all workspaces, visible. Through these meetings I also learned about an institution-wide movement of feminists to hold the university accountable for the barriers to women's success. A group of faculty, students, and staff met to create a document that outlined all the ways that the university maintained a system of inequality. Although Tanzanian institutions have widely embraced the discourse of women's rights and equality, and women's participation in government and education has increased, these discourses and laws have done very little to challenge barriers and discrimination that women face and the ways in which women's knowledge systems, "despite being sidestepped and undermined by colonial and postcolonial projects," are legitimate centers of power and "have sustained the continent for many years" (Swai, 2009, p. 1).

Across the African region, feminist scholars have spent more than 30 years working collaboratively with writers and activists at different locations on the continent to build an intellectual community, around shared goals such as strengthening the feminist politics of gender studies in African universities. According to Amina Mama, and confirmed by my first-hand experiences, there are many challenges to this kind of work. Mama (2010) states that, "systemic challenges arise from the domination of global policy arenas by narrow neo-liberal discourses that uncritically privilege the role of the market in driving development." Adding to this are unstable and undemocratic national and local political environments, which pose serious challenges to academic freedom and constrain intellectual cultures through intimidation and censorship. This type of environment may lead to scholars censoring themselves, and avoiding discussions, teaching, and research of potentially contentious issues. As I mentioned earlier, I was made aware of this potential while teaching a research methods in development course and introduced various possible topics and methods. Students responded with alarm and fear; they suggested that their fear was not unfounded (Mama & Iman, 1994; Sall, 2000).

Based on the experiences of my students in my first PAR workshop and through our informal meetings it became clear that students needed a way to connect with other African scholars to talk about doing research and how their identities intersected with this research. We used the materials from the AGI to assist us in creating additional workshops, research proposals, and projects, and building a community of feminist scholars. Feminist research is necessarily activist in nature and activist research is premised on a politics of solidarity.

An activist research ethic demands that we not only defy the academic canon by *not* maintaining distance, but actually go a great deal further, to actively relate to and engage with "research subjects" and explore ways of joining them and supporting their struggles. However, this ethic of solidarity demands a high degree of self-awareness and reflexivity. It requires that we take careful cognizance of our own subjectivity—manifest in our multiple positioning as political, institutional, ethnicized, gendered, sexualized, and classed subjects from particular locations.

Feminist Ujamaa

The first president of Tanzania (post-independence) was Mwailmu Julius Nyerere, from 1961 until he retired from office in 1985. Mwalimu is teacher in Kiswahili. Nyerere was called mwalimu because he was a teacher prior to joining politics. Nyerere developed a version of African socialism called *ujamaa,* or familyhood, that formed the basis of cultural, social, and economic development. The idea was that Nyerere created the basis of a uniquely African socialism after noting the limitations of a Marxist-based socialism and his belief that the implementation of this type of socialism was not appropriate for Tanzania or Africa. Ujamaa has many dimensions but hinges on the idea *that a person becomes a person through the community.* Despite the failings of ujamaa as an economic system, ujamaa as a uniting principle still holds a lot of power. As I searched for ways to be a part of a community in Dar es Salaam, I slowly began to realize that what was privileged in the expatriate communities—my job, education, and life as an individual—really had little influence in other settings.

Mohanty argues that differences between people are never just "differences"—"in knowing differences and particulars we can better see connections and commonalities because no border or boundary is ever complete or rigidly determining" (Mohanty, 2003, p. 505). The object is to understand how "specifying difference allows us to theorize universal concerns more fully" (Mohanty, 2003, p. 505). Far from erasing difference, the feminist solidarity model uses its historical basis to find areas of connection between women in diverse communities that can be translated into political activism. Using the perspective of a "cross cultural lens" enables an anti-globalization position that focuses both on substantive issues of exploitation and sites of resistance and struggle.

What I experienced—the community that developed over the meals shared, the workshops hosted, the conversations had—were all examples of what I describe as *feminist ujamaa*—a sort of family we shared through our commitments to each other through feminism, especially African feminisms. Many of my students were not from Dar es Salaam and had to live far from their families and children in order to receive an education. Our community offered the women involved a way to survive and navigate the challenges of being a woman on campus. We created a community of resources to succeed as students, researchers, and future practitioners. Feminist ujamaa offers us a transnational model of solidarity that is neither rooted in Eurocentric, androcentric history, notions of community, or individuality. Rather, feminist ujamaa requires knowledge of both the mechanisms of the global; an attention to women's history, activism, and legal rights; as well as an attention to the specificity of lived experience—especially as made possible through the nation and culture. Our community was both virtual and local, using the power of technology to bring our voices together into dialogue.

In this chapter I explore various aspects of feminist education abroad, feminist models of transnational solidarity, using community based pedagogy, and the educational power of creating and privileging community. Ultimately, I suggest all are essential elements in meaningful, transformative education and social justice work. Although we give a lot of lip service to the idea that transnational work is essential for our students, rarely do we demand this of ourselves. My time teaching at UDSM was the most challenging of my life, but it was also the source of my greatest rewards. Never have I experienced that type of familyhood through community, especially in the U.S. academy where I had traditionally been removed from my family and community. For me, *feminist ujamaa* is the expression of the complications of life at the intersections of family, community, gender, and the transnational.

REFERENCES

Barker, T. S., & Smith H. W. (1996). A perspective of a new taxonomy for international education. *International Education, 26*, 40–55.

Barnes, T. (2007). Politics of the mind and body: Gender and institutional culture in African universities. *Feminist Africa 8*. Retrieved from http://www.feministafrica.org

Bennett, J. (2002). Exploration of a gap: Strategising gender equity in African Universities. *Feminist Africa 11*. Cape Town, South Africa: African Gender Institute.

Berry, H. A., & Chisholm, L. A. (1999). *Service-learning in higher education around the world: An initial look*. New York: The International Partnership for Service-Learning.

Campt, T. (2011). What's the "trans" and what's the "national" in transnational feminist practice—A response. *Feminist theory & activism in global perspective: Feminist review conference proceedings*, e130–e135.

Code, L. (2000). How to think globally: Stretching the limits of imagination. In U. Narayan & S. Harding (Eds.), *Decentering the centre: Philosophy for a multicultural, postcolonial and feminist world* (pp. 67–79). Bloomington, IN: Indiana University Press.

Collins, P. (1990). *Black feminist thought: Knowledge, consciousness and the politics of empowerment.* Boston, MA: Unwin Hyman.

Crabtree, R. D. (2008). Theoretical foundations for international service learning. *Michigan Journal of Community Service Learning,* 15(1),18–36.

Crabtree, R. D., Sapp, D. A., & Licona, A. C. (Eds.). (2009). *Feminist Pedagogy: Looking Back to Move Forward.* Baltimore: Johns Hopkins University Press.

Dewey, J. (1938/1998). *Experience and education.* London: Macmillan.

Ferree, M. M. (2006). Globalization and feminism: Opportunities and obstacles for activism in the global arena. In M. M. Ferree & A. M. Tripp (Eds.), *Global feminism: Transnational women's activism, organizing, and human rights* (pp. 3–23). New York: New York University Press.

Freire, P. (1970). *Pedagogy of the oppressed.* New York: Continuum.

Gaidzanwa, R. (2007). Alienation, gender and institutional culture at the University of Zimbabwe. *Feminist Africa 8: Rethinking Universities.* Cape Town, South Africa: African Gender Institute.

Godkewitsch, N. V. (1997). *Development, popular education and feminisms: Mending the gap through praxis.* Unpublished thesis, Saint Mary's University, Canada. Retrieved January 28, 2012, from: http://proquest.umi.com.cyber.usask.ca/pqdweb? did=738215331&sid=14&Fmt =6&clientId=12306&RQT= 309&VName=PQD

Hanson, C. L. (2006). *Toward transformative learning and a transnational feminist pedagogy: Experiences of activist-facilitators working in development.* Unpublished dissertation, The University of British Columbia, Canada. Retrieved January 28, 2012, from: https://circle.ubc.ca/bitstream/handle/2429/7103/ubc_2009_spring_hanson_cynthia.pdf?sequence=1

Hartman, D., & Roberts, B. (2000). Overview: Global and local learning: The benefits of international service learn- ing. *Metropolitan Universities,* 11(1), 7–14.

hooks, b. (2003). *Teaching Community. A pedagogy of hope,* New York: Routledge.

hooks, b. (1994). *Teaching to transgress: Education as the practice of freedom.* New York: Routledge.

Ifekwunigwe, J. O. (1998). Borderland feminism: Towards the transgression of unitary transnational feminisms. *Gender and History,* 10(3), 553–557.

Jaksch, M. (2003). In Zimmerman, E., Grauer, K., & Irwin, R. (Eds.). *Women Art Educators V: Conversations Across Time (pp* . . Reston, VA: National Art Education Association.

Kaplan, C. (1994). The politics of location as transnational feminist practice. In I. Grewal, & C. Kaplan (Eds.), *Scattered hegemonies: Postmodernity and transnational feminist practices* (pp. 137–152). Minneapolis, MN: University of Minnesota Press.

Lather, P. (1991). *Getting Smart: Feminist Research and Pedagogy within/in the Postmodern.* New York: Routledge.

Mama, A. (1995). *Women's studies and studies of women in Africa.* Dakar: CODESRIA.

Mama, A. (2005). Gender studies for Africa's intellectual transformation. In T. Mkandawire (Ed.), *African intellectuals: Rethinking politics, language, gender and development.* London.

Mama, A. (2011). What does it mean to do feminist research in African contexts? In A. Smith, *Feminist theory & activism in global perspective: Feminist review conference proceedings,* pp. e4–e20.

McCallon, M., & Holmes, B. (2010). *Faculty-led 360: Guide to successful study abroad*. Agapy LCC.

Mohanty, C. T. (2003). *Feminism without borders: Decolonizing theory, practicing solidarity*. Durham, NC: Duke University Press.

Naples, N. A., & Desai, M. (2002). *Women's activism and globalization: Linking local struggles and transnational politics*. New York: Routledge.

Nnaemeka, O. (2004). Nego-feminism: Theorizing, practicing, and pruning Africa's way. *Signs: Journal of Women in Culture & Society*, 29(2), 357–385.

Odejide, O. (2007). What can a woman do? Being women in a Nigerian University. *Feminist Africa 8: Rethinking Universities*. Cape Town, South Africa: African Gender Institute.

Oyewumi, O. (2003). *African women and feminism: Reflecting on the politics of sisterhood*. Africa World Press.

Sall, E. (Ed.). (2000). *Women in academia: Gender and academic freedom in Africa*. Dakar: CODESRIA.

Shrewsbury, C. (1987). Empowerment as pedagogy of possibility. *Language Arts*, 64, pp. 370–82.

Swai, E. (2010). *Beyond women's Empowerment in Africa: Exploring dislocation and agency*. Palgrave Macmillan.

Walkerdine, V. (1998). Daddy's Girl: Young Girls and Popular Culture. Harvard University Press.

14 Community and Family as Critical Sites for Transformative Education
Implications for Practice

Toby S. Jenkins

A FAMILY TREASURE CHEST

As previously shared, this book was motivated by a past study examining how college students of color define, understand, and articulate the utility of culture. As I began that original study, I found students to be somewhat intimidated by the word "culture." Being a part of an academic community, they associated culture with things like the idea of "high culture" (fine art) or as an interest of fields like anthropology that studied the intricate ethnographic details of culture and ethnicity. In either case, they did not see themselves as experts. I started the study at Penn State University and conducted it within our cultural center. During the very first interview session, the students sat comfortably in the library of the cultural center waiting for our interview session to begin. They were familiar with one another and talked amongst themselves about various topics—the upcoming sorority event that night and the activities of the past weekend. As I began the discussion and reiterated to them that this will be a group interview/dialogue on how they define culture, a hint of nervousness filled the room. Although students were aware of the topic and had voluntarily agreed to participate in the session, I observed some students sharing quick glances at one another with expressions that seemed to communicate, "What do I know about culture?" Other students, who were initially sitting upright as I called them to order, began to slump back in their seats seeming to prepare themselves to disengage from the conversation. These nonverbal clues suggested that perhaps the appropriate research question should have been, "Can students talk about their culture?" But one initial statement about family opened the floodgates of response and unlocked doors of interest among students. "I think family is a really big important part of my culture," Noland shares. "Yes, yes!" others chime in.

Over the course of 5 years and after interviewing over 100 college students, I found that many of the students who participated in the study, whether they were at an urban institution or a rural one, regardless of socioeconomic background or race, named family as the most significant component of anything cultural. The personal relationships between family and community friends established the foundation for their basic understanding of culture and served as the first point of reference for them to engage in critical thought and remembrance of their cultural histories. Their family structure was more of a community that included many people beyond their immediate parents and siblings. Family was a treasure chest of grandparents, other extended family members, neighbors, and unrelated friends of the family whom they still referred to as "aunt" or "uncle." These extended family networks were actively involved in helping to raise and care for them as children. The members of this community family helped to shape students' values and ethics by sharing with them important wisdom from their life experiences. But most importantly, these extended family members seemed to personify a cultural ethic of selflessness and generosity that was deeply appreciated by students. Undoubtedly, education must start with the world the student knows. This world is strongly tied to family bonds. Within their families, students come to understand how to navigate the outside world. And it is in the home that they develop their first understanding of the importance of education. The strong impact and importance of families reveals that the university should do more to include families in the educational life of students. What the students in this study point out is the need to have their real home communities understand and support their college experience. College adjustment is undoubtedly important. However, might we need to change our views of what healthy adjustment looks like? Could students possibly establish a both home and campus experience rather than being forced to adopt the either family or college philosophy? It seems that finding ways to merge these two worlds may help students to culturally transition into and out of college. For it is home where students most often immediately find themselves a few days after commencement and it is with their families that they will experience the rest of their lives.

COMMUNITY AND COLLEGE

In the past, scholars have often associated college success with the ability to acculturate into the college environment (the ways in which the student must change rather than how the university must change). Rendon, Jalomo, and Nora (2008) suggest that these theories were similar to research ideologies of the 1960s, which often dissected the behavior of the individual without taking into consideration the broader context of the institutional and social forces that impede success. They also assert that this approach failed to privilege the oppositional cultures and forms of community capital that prove to be valuable in the success of students. In other words, previous work had not acknowledged the importance and value of a student's cultural and community experience. Culture, community, and family are at the heart of citizenship and community commitment. In the classic text, *The Mis-education of the Negro*, Woodson

(1977) asserted that the Negro, at that time, lacked the faculties of critical thought about her community as well as the agency to create positive change within her cultural community because of the culturally oppressive lens through which she was educated.

Although many researchers and education activists have championed multicultural transformation within the policies, services, and ideologies of higher education institutions, still often many students feel that college pulls them further away from their culture and family instead of encouraging them to fully appreciate these life experiences (Jenkins, 2009). In my previous study, one of the key themes that emerged was the idea that a familial and communal value for education was a critical component of culture. Across racial, ethnic, and economic class, all of the participants voiced a strong commitment by their family to education and an expectation for them to attend college. Many of these students were the first in their families to attend college and they told stories of mothers and grandparents working extremely hard to get them to and through school. "By hell or high water," they were going to college (Jenkins, 2009). This book offered stories from individuals who come from many different familial and community situations. Although some of the authors in this book came from families with multiple generations of collegiate experience, many were similar to the students in my previous study as they were a part of the first generation in their family to attend college. So, I will spend a brief moment addressing the critical intersection of family, community, and being a first generation (FG) college student. For most families and particularly for first-generation families, college is seen as the ultimate goal. The sense of educational urgency within the family positions college as a coveted prize in the familial experience for first-generation students. Jehangir (2010) explains that particularly for students coming from immigrant families, the first marker of success in America is often measured by the educational experiences of their children. Having a child successfully attend college makes the hard and difficult sacrifices that come with leaving one's homeland worth it. And when examining the ways in which college participation in one generation of any oppressed group can completely change the outlook for subsequent generations these families are correct. Rodriguez (2001) calls this "switching the tracks." A college degree changes the possibility of what a future can be for the whole family. Research confirms that although many families of FG students may not possess a firm understanding of the college experience, they do possess a firm belief that they want their child to experience college (Jehangir, 2010; Rodriguez, 2001; Jenkins, 2009). Undoubtedly, more formal campus programs need to be created that educate parents on the college experience and their new role as a college parent. Families also have a stake. Jehangir (2010) states, "because FG students often become representatives and models for their communities, failure in school is not just their own to bear, but also a reflection of their families as well" (p.

26). And so, it is clear that from an early age, the seeds of "college" are initially planted with the intent of growing a family garden.

Although all students are expected to develop and change during their time in college, first-generation college students often find themselves having to change the core of who they are in order to successfully adjust (Rodriguez, 2001; Jehangir, 2010; Allen, 1992; Cabrera, et al., 2006; Pascarella, 2004). The pressure to shave off the old culture in order to adopt new forms of social and cultural capitol has an immediately negative effect on the student (through feelings of isolation, marginalization, and resentment) and a more long-term effect on the family and community (Shockley, 2005). The ways that socioeconomics and educational participation intersect make a college education much more than an individual pursuit. The education of youth should ultimately have a positive impact on societies, communities, neighborhoods, and families. But as I mentioned previously, often for students coming from working class or impoverished communities, they are encouraged to use their education to eventually become a part of and contribute to already viable middle class communities rather than helping to transform communities in need. Although oppression imposes constraints, a college education ultimately affords individuals with choices. Obtaining a "good job" as a result of a college education allows you a choice of where you will live, how you will live, and how you might spend the spare time that being a middle class professional affords. But these are much more than personal choices. Where you choose to live affects which schools will benefit from your tax dollars. It impacts which businesses (local or national) you will patronize. It impacts who will benefit from the simple consequence of being your neighbor. How you choose to live—embracing a materialistic oriented culture or embracing the idea of modesty and social service—impacts who benefits from your "extra" money, corporations or communities.

As mentioned in the Introduction, in recent years, a popular mantra for young people from underprivileged backgrounds has been the phrase, "making it out." The idea of making it out of the impoverished community communicates the desire to avoid getting caught up in a cycle of oppression—to experience a new opportunity through school or work and to ultimately elevate oneself from the bottom of society. As I prepared this book, I posted the following on my Facebook page: "Making it Out of the Ghetto. What does it mean? Should that be the dream?" Below are two responses:

> I think it's telling that everyone is trying to get out of the ghetto, and no one is trying to eliminate the ghetto. When people talk of "escaping" they are saying they have left the poverty . . . and subsequent ignorance and violence of the ghetto. Very rarely do they say, " I want to pull everyone out of the poverty." Trust me, I understand that's a daunting task. But at some point we have to start saying that it's unacceptable for anyone to live that way, and that just certain individuals being blessed to escape that circumstance isn't enough. —Bomani Armah

I've always struggled with the idea of my "making it out the ghetto." Many people talk about where I come from in a way that separates me from where I come from . . . that I am only here because I am smart, amicable, and resourceful. That is not necessarily true. We all have those family members that are very smart but just didn't get the same opportunities we were given. So many good things happened to me during my lifetime, whether it's the teachers I had, the friends I met along the way, or just chance that have allowed me to be where I am today. Perhaps making it "out" should come with less elitism than it carries these days . . . not that we are "special," but that we are a member of the community given life changing opportunities. Opportunities that we, who "made it out," should extend to others as well. —Dayo, African woman

This book calls us to re-evaluate the meaning and purpose of a college education. Is college a one-way street—toward a success that resides far away from the community of origin? During an interview at Rutgers University, a comment by an African American male student named Floyd illustrates that when students dig deep to find the love that they have for friends and family, it also helps them to balance the challenge between their cultural community and their college community:

A few of the dudes I grew up with, when I first started school and came home I didn't really talk to them like that. It's more like a mutual understanding. You don't have to like what I'm doing but you're not going to disrespect me in the same capacity. But now I try to encourage them also—you know what, you're at community college right now, or your trying to play ball, or whatever the case may be. You can make something of yourself. I try to serve as an example. Whatever stereotype you have about me because I went off to college and now I'm back at home I'm going to show you that I'm here for us as a people and we can all come up, rather than just being like forget you.

Mike, another African American young man, shakes his head steadily in agreement. His face is proud as he shares with the group:

I like going home. I feel better now. People look to me as a role model now which is kind of weird. I got a story. I was getting off of the bus, and I see two guys from my high school walking toward me. They go, "Oh what's up man, you still go to Rutgers. Oh man I wish I was there with you man." I say you can do the same thing I do. It happens all the time. Another time, I went back to my old high school and all of my friends were like oh he's going to Rutgers. They showed me all the love—felt like I was king for a little while.

The need persists to explore the role, responsibility, and social impact of college-educated children from all types of socioeconomic communities. Are students really aspiring to use their college education to raise up the community that raised them or is success seen as their ability to navigate their way away from the community? What makes this a pressing issue is that many community leadership scholars affirm that viable community change most often comes from within (Bynoe, 2004).

Both Jehangir (2010) and Rodriguez (2001) suggest that new and bold educational strategies such as the movement toward critical pedagogy (exploring race, class, gender, and power); re-constructionist multicultural education (transforming the whole educational process); and learning communities (collaborative learning tied to a shared living experience) offer important inroads toward change. Beyond educational programs that solely help students to navigate the new terrains of the college environment, truly significant learning requires the courage to create innovative educational experiences. Community-based cultural spaces may serve as intellectual spaces of inclusion for these students. Can the communities from which students come be considered as places of possibility (for significant learning, social change, and even post-collegiate success)?

CREATING SIGNIFICANT LEARNING OPPORTUNITIES IN COLLEGE

Integrating community-based cultural learning into the college educational experience requires a deep engagement of practices that underscore what Fink (2003) calls "Significant Learning." According to Fink (2003), significant learning differs from other types of learning because of its utility, urgency, and saliency in students' lives. One of the most defining factors is the way in which the educational experience motivates a change in the student. "For learning to occur, there has to be some kind of change in the learner. No change, no learning. And significant learning requires that there be some kind of lasting change that is important in terms of the learner's life" (Fink, 2003, p. 30). Fink is not talking about the types of change mentioned earlier such as assimilation and acculturation. In this case, the significant learning taxonomy refers to the ways in which education provides opportunities for students to come to know themselves more deeply, develop important attachments to the process of learning, connect what they learn to their lives, establish a sense of caring and commitment about a particular topic, and take action on what they have learned in some meaningful way. Through this work, my primary hypothesis is that by more creatively integrating family and community into the educational experience, more adequately including students' lived experiences as topics of intellectual discussion, and more frequently engaging students in community-based learning experiences, educational institutions might see meaningful change occur in the students' sense and appreciation of their culture, commitment to community activism, future aspirations, and overall appreciation for the purpose and experience of college. By significant learning, I am referring not only to initiatives that, through their structure and content, embody the types of learning included in the Fink Taxonomy, but I am also referring to experiences that embody a sense of innovation, creativity, and value for engaged scholarship through their location within the culture and within the community. In his book, *Scholarship Reconsidered: Priorities of the Professorate*, Boyer (1997) points out the growing need for colleges and universities to connect with communities in more meaningful ways:

> The scholarship of engagement means connecting the rich resources of the university to our most pressing social, civic and ethical problems, to our children, to our schools, to our teachers and to our cities. . . . I have this growing conviction that what's also needed is not just more programs, but a larger purpose, a sense of mission, a larger clarity of direction in the nation's life as we move toward century twenty-one. (p. 64)

The scholarship of engagement recognizes that not only do individual students need college, but communities also need college. They need the resources, talents, and skills that reside on a college campus and they need deep and creative thinkers who can work in partnership to help achieve community-based goals. But beyond this, colleges need communities. Scholars, researchers, teachers, and students have much to learn from mothers, fathers, and community elders. There is undoubtedly mutual benefit in the scholarship of engagement. The students in my prior study revealed their parents and grandparents to be more than family—they were also teachers. Colleges might benefit from looking at families in a different light. This might include inviting family members to facilitate workshops, serve as panelists, and lecture on campus. Or it might mean veering off the beaten path of traditional academic programming (lectures, brown bags) and creating safe, non-traditional and culturally affirming family/community events like family dinners, community storytelling circles, or sponsoring cultural "family vacations" by inviting families to attend cultural learning excursions and immersion trips. Whatever the shape this educational space might take, if we want to make our campus communities more cultural we must find creative ways to include rather than exclude families.

MASTER TEACHERS

The many perspectives, experiences, and stories in this book share one common thread—the sincere belief that our families were our greatest teachers. In Breanna's case, her father's life experience taught her the meaning of ambition; Ashley's neighborhood taught her the true meaning of community and diversity. Ed's father educated him on what it means to live a life of passion and purpose. Through the model of her lived experience, Crystal's mom was her first instructor on feminism. Beyond my father, many of my own family and community members taught me critical life lessons that now guide my actions. Susan Harris is my aunt. She was one of those favorite aunts. She was fun, she was caring, and she was incredibly generous. I always looked forward to spending Friday nights at her house—good times were guaranteed. But she wasn't just generous with her time. She also shared whatever money came her way. Her Christmas gift was always my favorite. This might seem superficial, but no one in our family was rich. To a kid from modest means, one special gift can mean a lot. What my Aunt Susan has taught is the importance of sharing your gifts: the value of sharing your joy, your spirit, and yes, even your material possessions. They can all leave lasting impressions on people's lives. Ms. Esther was the hair stylist in my neighborhood. What she taught me is that space is important. Ms. Esther ran a hair salon out of the "back room" in her house in South Carolina. Through her salon, she created a space that allowed folks to just talk. Hers was a gathering place for women young and old, to laugh, complain, tell stories, or vent frustration. She taught us that sometimes people simply need a space to remember their own voice. Our challenge as educators is to organically create such spaces of cultural safety. And finally, my mother taught me to imagine. She taught me the power and importance of imagination. She painted. She told stories. She wrote poetry. She made dresses. Out of scraps and out of thin air, she created beauty. She took us away from boring afternoons or scary thunderstorms to incredible lands that existed only in the imagination. Serving students is not simply about solving problems and fixing issues—it is also about carving out truly joyful, fun, creative, and engaging experiences in people's lives. It's about turning people's lives of struggle into fairytales or at least imagining that as a possibility. And ultimately this is the goal of my work. These people essentially gave me the foundation upon which my career has been built—college gave me the credential to pursue it. I am not suggesting that we all don't leave college having had life-changing educational experiences. The experiences inside of the college campus do transform us in meaningful ways. I just don't privilege it as more important than the life lessons gleaned from those master teachers who were the first to love our minds and nurture our hearts.

REFERENCES

Allen, W. (1992). The color of success: African-American college student outcomes at predominantly white and historically black public colleges and universities. *Harvard Educational Review*, 62(1) 26–44

Boyer, E. (1997). *Scholarship reconsidered: Priorities of the professoriate.* Jossey-Bass, San Francisco, CA p.64

Bynoe, Y. (2004). *Stand and deliver: Political activism, leadership, and hip hop culture.*
New York: Soft Skull Press.

Cabrera, A. F., Deil-Amen, R., Prabhu, R., Terenzini, P. T., Lee, C., Franklin, R. E. (2006). Increasing the college preparedness of at-risk students. *Journal of Latinos and Education, 5*, 79–97.

Fink, D. L. (2003). *Creating significant learning experiences: An integrated approach to designing college courses.* San Francisco: Jossey-Bass.

Jehangir, R. (2010). *Higher education and first-generation students: Cultivating community, voice and place for the new majority.* New York: Palgrave Macmillan.

Jenkins, T. (2009). A portrait of culture in a contemporary America. *NASPA Journal, 46*(2), 131–162.

Pascarella, E. T., Pierson, C. T., Wolniak, G. C., & Terenzini, P. T. (2004). First-generation college students: Additional evidence on college experiences and outcomes. *Journal of Higher Education, 75*, 249–284.

Rendón, L., Jalomo, R., & Nora, A. (2008). Theoretical considerations in the study of minority student retention in higher education. In J. M. Braxton, (Ed.), *Reworking the student departure puzzle.* Nashville, TN: Vanderbilt University Press. pp 56–70

Rodriguez, S. (2001). *Giants among us: First generation college graduates who live activist lives.* Nashville, TN: Vanderbilt University Press.

Shockley, K. G. (2008). Africentric education leadership: Theory and practice. *International Journal of Education Policy and Leadership 3*(3). Retrieved from http://www.ijepl.org.

Woodson, C. G. (1977). *The mis-education of the Negro.* New York: The Associated Publishers.

Contributors

Billy Brown is a native of the inner city of Atlanta, Georgia, and is most certainly an example of what is possible when determination and perseverance are part of one's character. Upon graduating from high school, Billy joined the U.S. Marine Corps, where he served for 14 years. The Marine Corps not only allowed Billy to further his education and travel the world, but it also gave him leadership training which would play an integral part of his future achievements. After 14 years of military service, Billy began a new journey in corporate America where he currently serves as a senior sales director in the financial services industry. Billy has been married to his wife, Greta, for 23 years. They have three children: Breanna, a fourth-year college student; Britney, a high school senior; and Jaden, who will be entering first grade this fall.

Breanna Brown is a senior electronic media major at Rensselaer Polytechnic Institute. Upon completing her undergraduate degree in the spring of 2013, she plans to further her education at Boston University. Her life goal is to become a writer of many mediums.

Aracelie L. Castro is a financial specialist for the U.S. Department of Defense. Prior to serving the DOD, she was a finance officer for the U.S. Army. Castro earned an MBA in international business from the University of Texas–San Antonio and a Consortium Institute of Management and Business Analysis Certificate.

Crystal Leigh Endsley is currently Visiting Assistant Professor in Africana Studies at Hamilton College. Previously she was an instructor in the Women's Studies Department at The Pennsylvania State University, University Park, Pennsylvania, where she also served as Interim Assistant Director for the Paul Robeson Cultural Center. Endsley completed her graduate studies at Penn State's main campus, where she earned a dual Ph.D. in women's studies and curriculum and instruction. She is internationally recognized as a spoken word artist, activist, and actor, performing and presenting workshops and lectures both in the U.S. and abroad.

Giovanna Bargh Fini was born on November 17, 1987, in Arlington, Virginia. She was raised in Vienna, Virginia, just outside the capital, Washington, DC, in the area where her parents grew up. She attended George Mason University in Fairfax, Virginia, earning her BFA with a concentration in graphic design. She worked for a year in Washington, DC after college before moving to Italy to marry her fiancé. She is now happily married, living in Venice and enjoying her new life in Italy.

Sondra Frank is the youngest of two children, and product of a single-parent household. She grew up and matriculated through the public school system in Montclair, New Jersey, where she feels her love of the arts, creative spirit, and vivid imagination were cultivated. Sondra is a graduate of Howard University's School of Business and currently works in chapter relations with a non-profit in northern Virginia.

Cynthia (Ce) Garrison is an eco-feminist and radical organizer. She is active in the fight to end the socially and environmentally destructive practice of mountaintop removal coal mining, specifically in Appalachia. She was a trainer for the West Virginia, Kentucky, Pennsylvania, Virginia caucus at PowerShift, the largest national youth environmental conference in the country. She has been an intern at the School for Conflict Analysis and Resolution working on the Undergraduate Experiential Learning Project, and she is currently an intern at the George Mason University Office of Sustainability, where she is working on the advancement of sustainable. Her passion is working with students, and she plans to pursue a career in community organizing around the environment and the rights of women.

Joan Marie Giampa is a native Washingtonian. Joan was born in Arlington, Virginia, in 1960. Joan earned a DA in community college education from George Mason University in 2012, an MFA in painting from the University of Maryland in 1998, and a BFA in graphic design from James Madison University in 1983. Currently she teaches at Northern Virginia Community College and George Mason University. Joan maintains an artist studio in historical downtown Vienna, Virginia, where she has lived for the past 40 years. She has four children: Giovanna, Jeremy, John Nicholas, and Aubrey.

LaChan V. Hannon is a teacher and educational advocate who, in 2007, co-founded the Greater Expectations Teaching & Advocacy Center for Childhood Disabilities (GETAC), a non-profit organization established to provide educational and advocacy services to children and parents of children with developmental disabilities. She has graduate certificates in autism and applied behavioral analysis and served as the director for a children's behavioral health and rehabilitative services program. LaChan is currently pursuing a master's degree in educational leadership/teacher leadership at The Pennsylvania State University. Her research and professional practice interests are grounded in developing novice and preservice teachers with skills to effectively support children with autism spectrum disorders and other special needs.

Michael D. Hannon is a National Certified Counselor and doctoral student in counselor education and supervision at The Pennsylvania State University, whose research informs counselors how to effectively serve counseling clients who live with and care for children with autism spectrum disorders. In 2007, he and his partner, LaChan Hannon, co-founded the Greater Expectations Teaching & Advocacy Center for Childhood Disabilities (GETAC), a non-profit organization established to provide advocacy and consultation services to parents of children with developmental disabilities. Mike spent 10 years working as a school counselor, college access adviser, and student affairs administrator before returning to school. He has maintained an active research agenda in the last several years and is the author or co-author of over 20 scholarly presentations, book chapters, and articles.

Ashley Hazelwood, M.Ed., received her bachelor's degree in education from Boston College and her master's degree in college student affairs from The Pennsylvania State University. Her research interests include but are not limited to retention of students of color, topics of access and equity, as well as the collegial experiences of women of color. Ashley is currently the Assistant Director of the Stevens Technical Enrichment Program (STEP), an office that works to support the holistic development of underrepresented students at Stevens Institute of Technology in Hoboken, New Jersey.

Marla L. Jaksch is an assistant professor of women's and gender studies at The College of New Jersey. Her research interests include transnational feminisms; gender and development; indigenous rights and grassroots organizing; gender and expressive/visual culture; cultural tourism, heritage, and preservation; feminist pedagogies and methodologies; and experiential learning. Jaksch has recently published pieces on hip hop in East Africa, women's expressive culture and sexuality on the Swahili coast, and women's contribution to the liberation struggle in Tanzania. She splits most of her time between the U.S. and Tanzania.

Sinitra N. Johnson is the director of the Upward Bound Program at Midlands Technical College in Columbia, South Carolina, and is a native of Laurens, South Carolina. She received a bachelor of science degree in criminal justice from the University of South Carolina and a master of education degree in guidance and counseling services from Clemson

University. Her motto is a quote from Marian Wright Edelman: *"Education is for improving the lives of others and for leaving your community and world better than you found it."* Sinitra has committed her professional career to assisting students in South Carolina gain access to higher education. Her student affairs interests include first-generation, low-income students and foster youth aging out of the foster care system and accessing higher education.

Anthony R. Keith, Jr. is a Washington, DC-area native who identifies as a poet, educator, and nerd. As a poet, Tony has traveled around the world teaching poetry and empowering young people to engage in the art of spoken word. As an educator, Tony has committed his life to working with first-generation, low-income, racial and ethnic minority students and engaging in cultural education and social justice programming on college campuses. As a nerd, his thoughts, writings, teachings, and performances are centered on topics dealing with race, gender, poverty, culture, and sexuality.

Edward J. Smith is a research analyst at the Institute for Higher Education Policy (IHEP), supporting the development and dissemination of research as well as providing project management in support of multiple organizational goals. In addition to his research experience in post-secondary access and success issues, Smith has a particular interest in culturally relevant classroom pedagogy and has taught courses in education policy studies, African and African-American studies, women's studies, and intergroup dialogue. Smith has also facilitated classes for support networks in the Davidson County Correctional Development Facilities (Nashville, Tennessee) and the Northeast Treatment Center (Philadelphia, Pennsylvania). Smith currently serves as an adjunct instructor in the English, ESL, liberal studies, public speaking, and world language program at the University of the District of Columbia, Community College.

Index